AMERICAN
POWERBOATS
The Great Lakes Golden Years

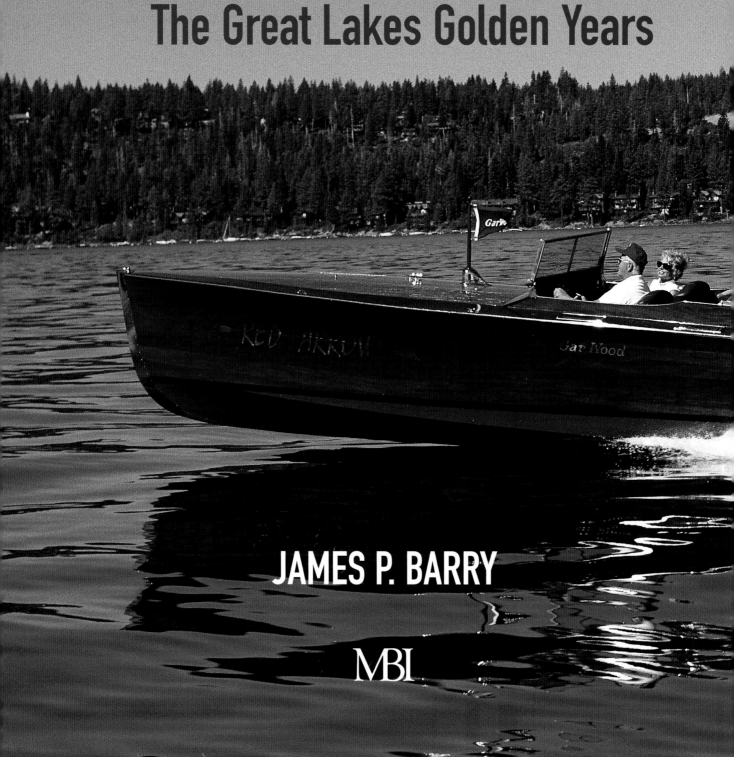

JAMES P. BARRY

MBI

Dedication

For Anne

This edition first published in 2003 by MBI, an imprint of
MBI Publishing Company, Galtier Plaza, Suite 200, 380
Jackson Street, St. Paul, MN 55101-3885 USA

MBI titles are also available at discounts in bulk quantity
for industrial or sales-promotional use. For details write to
Special Sales Manager at Motorbooks International
Wholesalers & Distributors, Galtier Plaza, Suite 200, 380
Jackson Street, St. Paul, MN 55101-3885 USA.

Library of Congress Cataloging-in-Publication Data Available

ISBN 0-7603-1466-7

On the front cover: A 1936 Seabird by the Port Carling Boat
Company. Although this company first produced simple
powered skiffs, it built triple cockpit runabouts by the
mid-1930s. *Classic Boating*

On the frontispiece: The control station on *Big Chief*, a 1929
Chris-Craft 38-foot commuting cruiser. *Classic Boating.*

On the title page: *Red Arrow,* a 33-foot Baby Gar from 1928.
It was Gar Wood's personal boat, and it still has its original
400 horsepower Liberty V-12 engine. *Classic Boating*

On the back, top: *Restless,* a 1930 Chris-Craft triple cockpit
racer. *Classic Boating.* **Bottom:** *Lady Helen* won the 1924
Junior Gold Cup race. She was a Hacker-designed
21-footer powered by a Scripps Junior Gold Cup 6.
Mystic Seaport, Rosenfeld Collection, Mystic, Connecticut.

Chapter 1, in slighty different form, appeared in *Inland
Seas®*

Edited by Amy Glaser
Designed by Mandy Iverson

Printed in China

CONTENTS

ACKNOWLEDGMENTS 6

INTRODUCTION 7

Chapter 1
BEGINNINGS 8

Chapter 2
POWERBOATS 16

Chapter 3
RUNABOUTS 46

Chapter 4
CRUISERS AND COMMUTERS 74

Chapter 5
COUNTDOWN TO FIBERGLASS 98

BIBLIOGRAPHY 120

INDEX 127

ACKNOWLEDGMENTS

This book depended heavily on the help others gave me. Those who contributed from their own knowledge were Conrad Adamski (Century), William T. Campbell Jr. (racing boats), Edna S. Johnson (Matthews), Tom Koroknay (Lyman), Ronald Lane (Defoe and Hacker), William T. Lindquist (Richardson and Rochester), Anthony J. Mollica Jr. (Gar Wood), Kevin Mowle (Gidleyford), and Leon R. Slikkers (Tiara). In addition, Marion Hacker Hurst, Tom Flood, and S. Steven McCready (Hacker) were very helpful. I also owe much background information to Gordon H. Millar, Warren S. Weiant III, and Bonnie W. Mark

Jack Savage and Jim Wangard helped guide the book to its publisher. Jim and Norm Wangard provided color photographs from *Classic Boating*. Gerald Farber was enthusiastic in providing photographs from his collection. C. Patrick Labadie allowed me to use his file of *Sail and Sweep* magazines.

Librarians, archivists, and curators have gone well beyond the call of duty to further my research. At the Antique Boat Museum, Clayton, New York, Phoebe B. Tritton, the reference librarian, constantly provided useful information, as well as several illustrations. Rebecca Hopfinger was helpful after Ms. Tritton's retirement. The Bay City, Michigan, Branch Library and its librarian, Lesley Hammond, supplied a great deal of material on boatbuilders of the area, especially the Defoe plants. The staff of the Benton Harbor, Michigan, Public Library provided Robinson Seagull information. I am also grateful to the Chicago Historical Society and the Chicago Public Library for material pertaining to that city. The Cleveland Research Center's Robert Murnan was unfailingly helpful, as was the staff of the Cleveland Public Library.

At the Dossin Great Lakes Museum in Detroit, John Polaczek guided me to material and provided photographs. Use of the archives at the Historical Collections of the Great Lakes, Bowling Green (Ohio) State University, was facilitated by its archivist, Robert Graham. The staff of the Huronia Museum in Midland, Ontario, and especially Director Jamie Hunter, guided me to Georgian Bay material.

The staff of the Inland Seas Museum, Vermilion, Ohio, and especially Martha Long, were exceptionally helpful. The Lake Erie Islands Historical Society and its curator, Edward W. Isaly, thoughtfully located material for me. Staff members at the Mariners' Museum of Newport News, Virginia, were always helpful in finding information, and John W. Pemberton of the museum was especially gracious in locating old photographs and arranging for their use. The Milwaukee Public Library's humanities coordinator, Virginia Schwartz, and the Wisconsin Marine Historical Society's director, Suzette J. Lopez, have been unfailingly supportive in the solution of many problems. At the Muskoka Lakes Museum in Port Carling, Ontario, Michael Thompson and Jan Hill graciously provided background material and photographs of Muskoka boats.

At Mystic Seaport in Mystic, Connecticut, the Rosenfeld Collection of photographs has recorded much of the history of recreational boating. Victoria R. Sharps has been a knowledgeable guide to the collection, and Peggy Tate Smith has been gracious in providing reproduction rights. Many other staff members of Mystic Seaport have been helpful. The New-York Historical Society provided background on the racing enthusiast Count Mankowski and his early death. The Parry Sound, Ontario, Public Library made its photograph collection available and granted permission to use some of the photographs. At Perry's Victory & International Peace Monument at Put-in-Bay on South Bass Island in Lake Erie, Director Gerald Althoff and Park Ranger Sue Judis kindly gave access to the memorial's collection of old local photographs and permitted me to use some of them. Tiara Yachts provided photographs and information about its products. The Toronto Harbour commissioners' archivist, Michele Dale, and the Toronto Port Authority archivist, Beth Tokawa, provided information and gave permission to use the photograph of the Toronto police boat.

Many consider the years between the two World Wars as the Golden Years of powerboating. Some, however, extend the period back to the beginning of the twentieth century, while others carry it forward to the start of fiberglass construction. A full history of powerboating, then, must cover the entire span—from about 1900 to 1960. During these Golden Years, Detroit was the center of auto development, while powered boats developed in its surrounding waters.

There, Gar Wood built the fastest racing boats in the world. Christopher Columbus Smith, whose first name was immortalized in the trademark Chris-Craft, built more fast pleasure boats than anyone else. John Hacker was the designer's designer, and his artistry in creating fast boats of many kinds is acknowledged today by the builders who still copy his work.

Lyman provided straightforward lapstrake boats that were popular in seafaring communities. The builder has gone, but the boats are still so popular that businesses have sprung up to refurbish them and keep them active. Matthews built power cruisers, and well-kept ones still exist. Enthusiasts spend winters aboard their Matthews in the Bahamas. More Richardson cruisers were owned throughout the country than any others. That boatbuilder has disappeared also, but owners cosset the remaining boats.

Century was a builder of some note. A restorer in Vermont, working on an old Century runabout, removed the dashboard of the boat. On the reverse side, written in yellow chalk, was "Figure this out, you son of a bitch." A challenge over time from one of the original builders to the next person who took the boat apart? The restorer might certainly have thought so.

Initially writing for a French audience, Gérald Guétat described North America as having "great rivers and immense lakes linked to one another by broad navigable waterways made this country a paradise for devotees of pleasure boating." The products that developed in that paradise quickly spread. Following the pattern of cars, a steady stream of boats was shipped to the East Coast, along the Ohio and Mississippi Rivers, and to the Gulf and Pacific Coasts. Boats went to the many small inland lakes.

John Hacker designed and built an express cruiser for use on Lake Tahoe. Farther afield, Gar Wood raced his boats in Europe, and word of his exploits spread. Chris-Craft provided runabouts of a one-design racing class for Riviera sportsmen and sold its stock boats widely abroad. John Hacker corresponded with people in over a hundred countries, sent them plans or boats, and produced a 38-foot commuter for the King of Siam. A Matthews boat crossed the Atlantic and then went on to Russia.

Boats from the Great Lakes area often traveled far in illustrious company. Over the years, Chris-Craft alone produced tenders carried aboard some 30 yachts whose hailing ports ranged from Detroit to London and Paris, and many ventured into far distant harbors where they lay at anchor while the tenders carried people ashore.

Boatbuilders did not cluster around Detroit as tightly as the auto manufacturers did. They could be found from the Thousand Islands, where Lake Ontario drains into the St. Lawrence, to Chicago and Duluth. They were located on the Muskoka Lakes just east of Georgian Bay, and on the Wisconsin lakes. The Detroit influence was felt throughout the builders. They used engines built or inspired by Detroit. Increasingly, those that grew and survived used mass-production methods drawn from auto manufacturing, and Detroit influenced the looks of their products.

When car windshields went from vertical to sloped in the 1930s, so did boat windshields. Between the Great Depression and World War II, designers of everything from refrigerators to wheelbarrows rounded off the corners and called the results "streamlined." Car designers led the move. They worked in one area where smoother lines had some real effect on increased speed. The appearance of speed was just as important to them as speed itself. The designers of boat exteriors followed, sometimes to excess. The designs of those boats may now be called Art Deco, especially if they still are pleasing to us.

Today, enthusiasts restore old motorboats and gather at old boat shows. Dedicated builders still make wooden boats. Specialized magazines are devoted to them, and there are clubs to support them. On almost any large body of water, one can find restored or replica wooden boats. The interest in powerboats of the Golden Years continues to grow and spread.

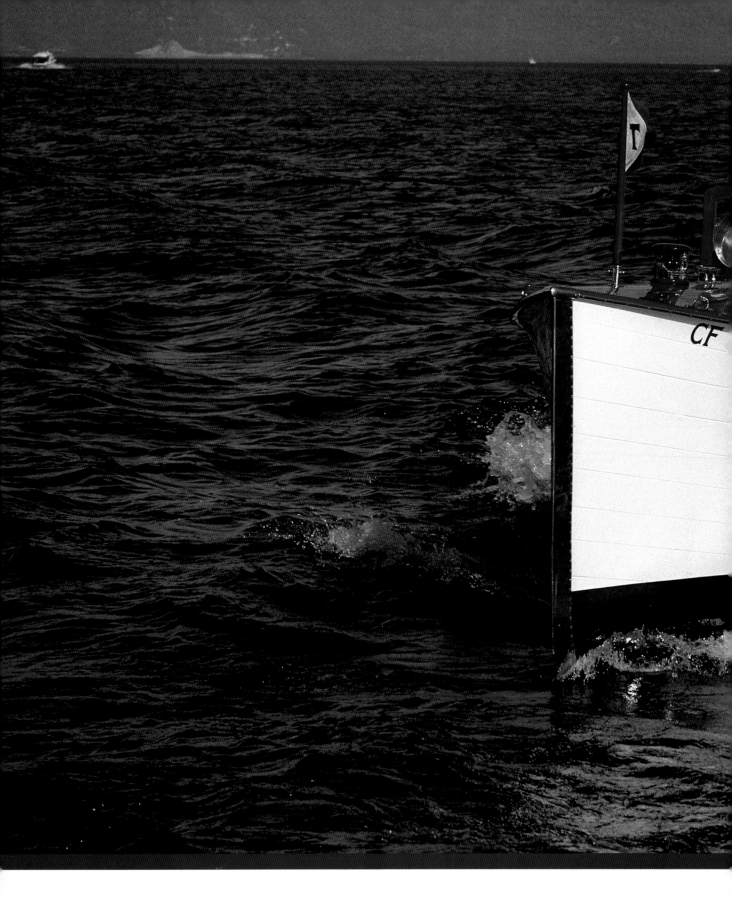

CHAPTER 1
BEGINNINGS

In 1898 the Racine Boat Company built the 72-foot steel *Hathor* for use on Lake Geneva in Wisconsin. *Hathor*, owned by the founder of Ryerson Steel, provided day cruises for such guests as Henry Ford, John D. Rockefeller, and Harvey Firestone. Originally steam driven, an in-line Lathrop six now powers the boat. *Classic Boating*

Beginnings

The central lakes of North America, where powerboats first would be mass-produced, saw the gradual development of powered small watercraft that ended in the burst of energy that affected both automobiles and boats in the first part of the twentieth century.

Steam Launches

In the 1880s a few comparatively small steamers built for personal use appeared in the Great Lakes region. The Herreshoff Manufacturing Company of Bristol, Rhode Island, built a 95-footer and delivered it to Mark Hopkins of St. Clair, Michigan, in 1882. For reasons one can only surmise, the same builder delivered a 100-footer to the same owner the next year. A Herreshoff 98-footer went to H. H. Warner of Rochester, New York, in 1882. These boats were so large that they could hardly be called launches; they no doubt had cabins, and today would certainly be considered yachts. Their size required paid crews, and thus they could easily operate despite a legal restriction put on all pleasure steam craft in the United States. The law stated that a steam launch, whatever its size, could only be operated when a licensed steam engineer was on board. Earlier and bigger steam boilers blew up occasionally, so there was some reason for the rule, although there is no record that the smaller and more advanced launch engines ever exploded. Rules in Canada were more temperate, and for that reason, steam launches were more common there.

In the United States, the examination for a steamer license was said to be not too difficult. Before applying, however, the would-be engineer had to have fired a steam boiler for two years. One of the few amateurs to achieve a license was Rosamund Burgess. Her husband, Starling Burgess, was a noted East Coast boat designer and builder. She served her apprenticeship firing the *Ox*, their boat that was used for general light towing of pleasure craft and family recreation.

Naphtha Launches

The law was eventually removed, but not until boats with other motive power had almost superseded steam

PREVIOUS PAGE: *Hickory*, a 28-foot launch built by Miller on the upper St. Lawrence River around 1910, was made of cedar on oak frames. *Classic Boating*

The steamer *Naiad*, built in 1890, was owned by W. E. Sanford, a Canadian businessman and senator. Sanford, whose duties often took him to England, said that he had Queen Victoria's permission to copy her royal yacht, although his boat was considerably smaller at 68 feet long. *Naiad* had one-piece steel frames tied together by a steel sheer strake, a steel stringer, and the steel keelson. The outer keel, stern post, and stem were white oak. Planking was fir, and was replaced with oak in 1896. *Naiad* was used on Lake Rosseau in the Muskokas for almost 50 years. *Muskoka Lakes Museum*

Ida, a normal steamer, carries a picnic party on Georgian Bay. Steam launches were seen more often in Canada than in the United States because U.S. regulations required that only licensed engineers could operate steam crafts. *Parry Sound Public Library J.B.M. 80*

launches. The first to supersede was the naphtha launch, usually just called the naphtha. In 1885 the Gas Engine & Power Company of New York City built the first naphtha under patent (the company soon became part of the giant firm known as Consolidated). The naphtha gained snob appeal through sales to European aristocrats, although one owner was Christopher Columbus Smith, a boatbuilder from Algonac, Michigan, who later gave his name to Chris-Craft. In general appearance the naphtha was much like the steam launch. It was up to 30 feet in length with a narrow hull surmounted by a fringed awning from bow to stern. Unlike the steam launch, which usually had boiler and stack amidships, the naphtha's machinery and stack were more compact and usually were at the stern. Most naphtha launches had polished brass boilers and stacks, which because of their similarity—though they were considerably larger—were sometimes called "samovars." An early auxiliary sailing cruiser had a naphtha engine. The naptha engine was more compact than the usual steam engine and used liquid fuel. Most steam launches, until late in their day, used wood or coal.

The naphtha engine was an external combustion engine, first patented in 1883. The patent said that it was to

A naphtha engine in a family boat at Put-in-Bay, Ohio, on Lake Erie. Naphtha launches used naphtha—an early form of gasoline—for both the flame under the boiler and the expanding fluid in the boiler but did not require licensed engineers. *Perry's Victory & International Peace Memorial, Put-in-Bay, Ohio*

BELOW: A replica naphtha launch, *Anita,* at the Antique Boat Museum in Clayton, New York. *Antique Boat Museum*

be operated on naphtha or stove gasolene [sic], "as the two are identical except in name." Some early references to naphtha engines called them "gasolene" engines. When internal combustion engines became common, it led to possible confusion. Naphtha was used as the fuel under the boiler and also as the expanding fluid in the boiler to drive the engine. In other words, it boiled gasoline. When the regulators became aware of the popularity of naphtha-driven boats, the internal combustion engine was coming along quickly, and they decided to regulate both kinds, as well as the steamers. A general rebellion on the part of boat owners and builders, all of whom complained vehemently to their legislators, stopped the move.

Gasoline Launches

In 1884 at San Francisco, the Union Gas Engineering Company put what generally is considered to be the first practical internal combustion marine engine in the United States into a motorboat. Union's affiliated engine builder, Globe of Philadelphia, added a marine engine to its line in 1885. The company pointed out that no license was needed to operate it, and for the following three years, the business doubled, redoubled, and redoubled again.

The California development sparked a wide production of engines. Many builders offered a heavy, single-cylinder engine that commercial fishermen and other nautical workers quickly adapted for their small boats used in almost every coastal and inland location. These "one-lung" engines were simple and easily maintained.

The first internal combustion engines for pleasure craft were lighter and smaller than the commercial applications. Users usually started their engines by manually turning the flywheels, either directly or by some sort of starting device, usually in the form of a crank. The boats the engines were installed in looked at first much like the steam launches and naphthas. They tended to be long and thin, or "toothpick" in shape, and most often had fantail sterns. Up to 30 feet or so, they generally were open or had the typical awning with fringed edges above a slim hull. Beyond that length they often bore cabins, but the hulls remained narrow.

Kahlenberg Engines

One engine builder was the Kahlenberg shop at Two Rivers, Wisconsin, where there was a fleet of sailing Mackinaw fish boats, each about 35 feet long. In 1898 John LaFond, a local fisherman, prevailed on machine-shop owners William and Otto Kahlenberg to build and install a one-cylinder, two-stroke engine in his boat. William is credited with designing and building the engine, which could

run backward so there was no need for clumsy reverse gears. Soon other fishermen followed LaFond's lead, and the Kahlenberg engines became known throughout the Lakes. They were beautifully made and highly reliable. Builders and owners also installed them in pleasure boats.

Electric starters were not yet invented. Workboat engines often were too heavy to be started using muscle power to turn their flywheels. One solution was to make them as "hot heads," built with a rod that extended into each cylinder head from outside and that was heated by a blow torch until it became red hot. Then gasoline under 30 pounds of air pressure was squirted into the cylinder, and the powerplant started. The tolerances in the fit of some of the early engines not built by Kahlenberg were scarcely ideal. The machines often exuded so many fumes that they could only be used in open boats.

Bigger engines for bigger boats followed, and by 1911 the brothers reorganized and enlarged their business. In 1912 they produced the first Kahlenberg semi-diesel—it started on gasoline, then switched over to fuel-injected oil. Although they also built engines for pleasure boats, the firm was off on a career of building heavy-duty commercial engines that in time were exported throughout the world.

Power Lifeboats

The first motor lifeboat for the U.S. Life Saving Service was tested at Marquette, Michigan, on Lake Superior, in 1899. The two-cylinder, 12-horsepower engine was provided by the Lake Shore Engine Works of Marquette. Keeper Henry J. Cleary of the Marquette station and Lieutenant C. H. McLellan of the Revenue Cutter Service—who was a researcher in lifesaving equipment for the Revenue Service's secondary mission of rescue—tested the boat in Lake Superior storms. They were sufficiently impressed and recommended its adoption to a commission headed by Professor C. H. Peabody of the Massachusetts Institute of Technology. The commission recommended that the Life Saving Service adopt power lifeboats, and gradually that was done.

Pleasure Boats

The Racine Boat Manufacturing Company of Racine, Wisconsin, published a catalog in 1901. That catalog has one of the best presentations of recreational powerboats of the early twentieth century. The early pages show a series of the company's steam yachts. The smallest was a 65-footer. The steam launches were next, and only a single specimen was shown. After that there was a wide selection of "Twentieth Century electro-vapor launches," which the builders obviously considered the next popular thing because those launches occupied most of the catalog.

White Cap, built in the early 1900s in Algonac, Michigan, is on display at a modern boat show. *Classic Boating*

The text explains that electro-vapor motors spray a vapor of common gasoline into a cylinder, where an electric spark ignites it. These motors were what soon became known as internal combustion engines. (Racine's name was perhaps a better one than "gasoline explosive engines," also an early usage.) The catalog lists the advantages of boats thus powered: "No government restrictions, no licensed engineer or pilot, no smokestack, no fire, no noise from exhaust. No naphtha under pressure." The writer of that passage might be surprised by the noises from the exhausts of some of the descendants of those launches, but his engines were clearly superior to their predecessors. The boats ranged from 15 to 52 feet; the latter was "a thoroughly safe, reliable cruising launch" that had a beam of 11 feet, 6 inches. The speed given for a 15-footer was 6 miles per hour; for a 30-footer and a 40-footer, 10 miles per hour.

Those who wanted greater speed faced a problem. All boats at this time had displacement hulls, which pushed their way through the water. Planing hulls that rode on top of the water were still in the future. Generally, the narrower the beam of a displacement boat in relation to her length, the faster she was expected to go. Except for the most extreme racing boats, this rule had to be tempered by considerations of general usefulness and seaworthiness.

The *Geisha*, one of the leading racing boats of the day, achieved a top speed of 19 miles per hour.

Hull Forms

The Rudder magazine, the bible of recreational boat owners of that time, published plans and photographs of many boats, and designers worked to produce faster craft. The traditional fantail stern tended to squat at speed, so designers searched for the best stern shape to go above a whirling propeller. They used counter stern, cruiser stern, sharp stern; or transoms V-shaped, flat, angled, or curved. There were numerous combinations. In 1901 the magazine published plans for a 27-foot launch designed by Fairbanks-Morse of Chicago. The boat had a canoe stern; two single-cylinder engines powered it, and each drove its own propeller.

A form that contributed to later V-bottom boats also began to appear. Such a boat was generally very narrow and looked something like a knife on edge, with a sharp bow intended to slice easily through the water and a hull in the shape of a deep V.

Detroit

In April 1901 *The Rudder* magazine commented, "Although naphtha or gas engines are now found in most of

A 35-foot Racine internal combustion launch from 1901. *Milwaukee Public Library/Wisconsin Marine Historical Society*

Arrow is an early displacement runabout of the knife-on-edge type, on Georgian Bay. *Parry Sound Public Library M.B.178*

the power-driven craft, there are still a few men who prefer steam as the most thoroughly reliable of all motive powers," but steam launches were fast disappearing. Builders pioneered light internal combustion engines of more complex design for faster boats; a number of them were attracted to Detroit's automotive culture. Among them was the Van Blerck Motor Company. Joseph van Blerck had come from Holland to the United States and was drawn to Detroit, where he helped design the engine that went into Ford's Model T, and then began his own company that, in time, dominated the pre–World War I market for speedboat engines. At the other extreme, the first production outboard motor, the Waterman, was built in Detroit in 1905.

Detroit and its environs at the end of the nineteenth and beginning of the twentieth centuries had become the equivalent of Silicon Valley. Young geniuses who wanted to create better engines and put them into better vehicles flocked to the city. Most of them knew each other, and many changed from job to job, often intent on launching their own companies. New and startling ideas, such as mass production, proliferated, were tested, and then were accepted or forgotten. They raced cars and strived to make them faster. The major interest of these men was automobiles, but the great burst of energy spread to every possible application of power. The Great Lakes and their tributaries surrounded Detroit, and installing faster engines into faster boats was an obvious step.

CHAPTER 2
POWER BOATS

Baby Reliance from 1912. *Chris-Craft Collection, Mariners' Museum, Newport News, Virginia*

Racing Boats

By 1916 *Miss Detroit* had twice represented her city in the Gold Cup races. She was "a broken, battered hulk after the [last] race, fit only for junk," but the syndicate that owned the boat still owed the designer-boatbuilder $1,800. The syndicate decided that it had to sell her to clear as much as it could. Lee Barrett, the secretary of the syndicate, stood up in the lunchroom of the Detroit Exchange Club and pled for some loyal Detroiter to buy her. There was silence. Then a slim, dark-haired, modest fellow about 35 years old stood up in the back of the room. "How much do you want for the boat?"

Barrett thought the man didn't look as though he could pay $1,800 for anything. He leaned over to a judge sitting beside him. "Shall I tell him the price?"

"Sure," the judge said. "Take a chance." Barrett told the man the price.

"I've got $1,000," he responded. "I'll give you a six-month note for the balance."

Barrett consulted the judge again. "Is his note good for $800?"

"His word is good for a million," said the judge.

The deal was done, and millionaire Garfield A. Wood entered the scene.

Gar Wood went to Algonac, Michigan, to see the boat. She was at the boat-building plant of Chris Smith, who had a small operation and was grateful to get back his $1,800. Wood went further and bought a controlling interest in the plant. He immediately started to build *Miss Detroit II*.

Wood had been attracted to powerboats all of his life. He didn't have enough money to indulge in his hobby until he invented the basic mechanism for a dump truck. In a day when coal trucks delivered coal to almost every business and household, his invention soon made him a rich man. Gar Wood Industries, run efficiently by Gar's brother, Logan Wood, produced that invention and others, ranging from road machinery to furnaces.

Miss Detroit II used the Sterling engine from the previous boat, but everything else was new. The boat's design was by Chris Smith. Smith always used the time-honored design method of carving a half-model of the boat, rather

PREVIOUS PAGE: The 33-foot *Baby Gar IV*, a reproduction of Gar Wood's 1924 winning racer. *Classic Boating*

than laying out the design on a drawing board. He had already built a single-step hydroplane in order to escape the patents held by an American designer living in Europe who had devised a more complicated multistep method.

Chris Smith's Early Racers

A man with an amiable, lumpy face and an addiction to cigars, Chris Smith had built race boats since 1910. That year he had made the first one for the flamboyant Baldy Ryan, who had joined him in the Smith-Ryan Boat Company. *Reliance III* was the third boat that was made for Ryan and is said to be the first Smith hydroplane. Ryan raced that boat successfully with Jay Smith, one of Chris' sons, who served as mechanic ("mechanician" in the words of the day) of the two-man crew. Ryan, the company's chief salesman, sold a boat to J. Stuart Blackton, the owner of the Vitagraph motion picture company. Ryan guaranteed it would go faster than 40 miles per hour (the record then was 34.66 miles per hour).

As Smith worked on Blackton's boat, his mechanical department went to work on the engine. Smith and Ryan had chosen a 250-horsepower Van Blerck, made in Detroit. Jack Beebe, their head engine man, lightened it. He bored holes through the connecting rods and cut out pieces of iron elsewhere and substituted a lighter metal. When the engine went into the hull, the result was the first *Baby Reliance*, which was only 20 feet long. Blackton entered her in an exhibition race on Gravesend Bay, off Brooklyn, New York. In a preliminary trial run on a foggy day, he opened her up. She went a lot faster than 40 miles per hour and at top speed struck the wake of a passing steamer. She promptly sank and Blackton and Smith were left paddling in water and fog until a passing ferry saw them and picked them up.

Undaunted, Blackton commissioned the Smith-Ryan firm to build him two more racers, *Baby Reliance II,* 20 feet long, and *Baby Reliance III,* 26 feet long. With Ryan and Jay Smith aboard, they swept the races in 1912. The 20-footer won first in the 20-foot class, then in the 26-foot class, the 32-foot class, and the 40-foot class. As Lee Barrett later put it, "They almost ruined powerboat racing in America." Smith, Ryan, and Blackton then brought out *Baby Reliance*

Baby Speed Demon from 1914. *Chris-Craft Collection, Mariners' Museum, Newport News, Virginia*

Christopher Columbus Smith at the 1919 Gold Cup race.
Mystic Seaport, Rosenfeld Collection, Mystic, Connecticut

III and, over an officially measured mile, ran at 53.7 miles per hour to set a new record.

Blackton entered the race for the Harmsworth, the British International Trophy, and had the boats shipped to Huntingdon Bay on Long Island, the race's location. *Baby Reliance II* completed the first heat of the Harmsworth far ahead of the pack. Bernard Smith, a son of Chris, was the driver, and Wallace Pugh was mechanic. The light hydroplane was not well suited to open water, which lay at the northern end of the course. During the second heat when the boat was leading by a mile, spray shorted out the magneto and the engine stopped.

After the race, Ryan, cocky as ever, went aboard the yacht of Sir E. Mackay Edgar, put a check for $20,000 on the table, and challenged Edgar to a race the following spring on the Thames in England. Edgar accepted the bet, but the race never occurred. Ryan, a high-stakes gambler with horses and cards, as well as boats, was broke within six months. Shortly afterward Smith and Ryan dissolved their partnership.

John L. Hacker's Early Racers

In 1903 John L. Hacker of Detroit designed *Au Revoir*, a boat that *Motor Boat* magazine called "the fastest boat of her size and power in this country." He followed with several winning racers named *Kitty Hawk* in the early 1900s. In 1911 Hacker's *Kitty Hawk II* won a challenge race in Atlantic City against a local boat named *Sand Burr II*, leading *Motor Boat* to say that the boat now held the 26-foot championship of the country. Hacker designed the *Oregon Kid*, a small racing boat. It was built on the Pacific Coast in 1913 and won nearly every race she entered. In early usage anything that planed on water was called a hydroplane, but this racer had a stepped bottom. Gar Wood said, "We never had a real hydroplane until Hacker brought out the *Oregon Kid.*"

Hacker also designed and built *Miss Los Angeles*, which won the Nordlinger Trophy on the Pacific Coast in 1919. In 1921 he designed and built *Adieu,* which won the Fisher Trophy. In 1922 his *Baby Sure Cure* became the fastest single-engine hydroplane when it reached a speed of 64.8 miles per hour in a race at the Chicago Regatta.

Early Gold Cup Races

The first race for the Gold Cup, which became the ultimate trophy in American powerboat racing, was held in 1904. (There were actually two Gold Cup races in 1904, and both were held on the Hudson River; the first, in June, drew so few contestants that a second was run in September, and 10 boats raced.) For the next nine years the cup was held by yacht clubs in the Thousand Islands area of the upper St. Lawrence River, just east of Lake Ontario, and the races were held in their home waters. At first a complex handicap system accommodated boats of many sizes and shapes. In 1908 handicapping was abolished. Contesting boats were close to pure racers. In 1910 the first planing boat, *Skit*, competed, but the day was windy and the water too rough, so she had to drop out. Finally, in 1911, a planing boat, *MIT II* built by Fitz Hunt, became the winner. In 1912 all entries were planing boats.

In 1913 an interloper, a 300-horsepower fast boat named *Ankle Deep*, representing the Lake George Racing Association in upstate New York, challenged the planing boats. Her owner, Count Mankowski, stood at the wheel, and a mask covered his face to protect him from the lash of the waters. *Ankle Deep* won the race handily and took away the cup, which never returned to the St. Lawrence.

The Count, an American citizen with an inherited title, was an exotic figure who appeared brightly though briefly in the history of boat racing. He was the son of a Polish nobleman and married to an American heiress. They lived at Bolton, New York, on Lake George during the summer and at various southern resorts in the winter. He died of typhoid fever in New Orleans in April 1917 at the age of 38.

The next year at Lake George, disaster overtook *Ankle Deep* during the third heat. "If Count Mankowski had not bounced his propeller off the floating log he himself would not have bounced out of *Ankle Deep* into the transparent waters of Lake George and the Countess would not have fainted," *Motor Boating* reported. Mankowski was not hurt. The race was won by *Baby Speed Demon II,* which carried the cup away to Manhasset Bay. Blackton won the 1914 Gold Cup with *Baby Speed Demon II,* the Smith-rebuilt *Baby Reliance III.*

Chris Smith's Dream Boat

Ryan had gone, but Blackton still bought boats from Smith. Blackton, however, found that World War I had shut off parts of Europe, especially Germany, from his movies, and he had to retrench.

There followed an oft-told story of Chris Smith. During the winter of 1914–1915 he went to New York to try to sell a boat to Blackton. He spent several unsuccessful days, and then he got into a poker game that stripped him down to his last seven cents. He received a telegram from Detroit, tipped the delivery boy the seven cents, and went to bed. He had a dream that a beautiful speedboat was on display in downtown Detroit and hundreds of equally beautiful flower girls were throwing baskets full of money into the boat.

A more skeptical soul—Blackton, perhaps—might have connected the dream with the old saw that a boat is a hole in the water into which you throw money. As Smith interpreted it, however, it meant that the people of Detroit would subscribe to a speedboat built in the name of the city. He borrowed $100 from a friend and hastened back to Detroit, where he told the idea to a group of civic leaders who liked it and formed the Miss Detroit Power Boat Association to raise the money. Smith went to work on the boat that became *Miss Detroit,* a single-step hydroplane powered by a 250-horsepower Sterling engine. When the boat was completed, it was shipped off to Manhasset Bay to contend for the Gold Cup.

Most of the good boats failed to compete for the Gold Cup because of one misfortune or another. *Miss Detroit*

The first *Miss America. Chris-Craft Collection, Mariners' Museum, Newport News, Virginia*

won because she had less trouble than any other boat. Just before the start of the race, the driver disappeared. The chairman looked around wildly at the Detroiters standing by. "Who knows how to drive a boat?" A freckle-faced kid named John Milot said he did. The chairman told Milot,

Packard Chriscraft, a 26-footer built by Smith, won the 1922 Gold Cup after the rules had been changed to exclude Gar Wood's powerful craft. *Chris-Craft Collection, Mariners' Museum, Newport News, Virginia*

Wild Horses is a modern interpretation of a 1921 John Hacker racer built with present-day techniques. It is powered by a Rolls-Royce V-12. *Classic Boating*

"Get in there and drive." Luckily, Jack Beebe, the mechanic, was in place. He tended to the engine, drove the boat, held on to Milot so that the young man wouldn't bounce overboard, and won the race. Beebe and Milot kept going around the course for two more laps before they could be signaled in—they had lost count of the laps.

The next year on the Detroit River, *Miss Detroit* faced a new competitor, *Miss Minneapolis*. She was built by

Smith and easily carried the Gold Cup off to Minneapolis. Then Gar Wood appeared, took *Miss Detroit II* to Minneapolis in 1917, and brought the Gold Cup back.

East versus Midwest

The distance between the East Coast and Detroit seems to be farther to an Easterner looking west than to a Detroiter looking east. By 1917 the Gold Cup had remained in the Midwest too long for the Easterners who had established the contest. A. L. Judson, president of the American Power Boat Association, said, "I'm going to bring the Gold Cup Trophy back East. That's where it belongs."

CF 3643 KX

light an engine as possible, and adapted such an engine for marine use. Wood's concept of speed under power, as Joseph Gribbins and Jay Higgins noted, was to "put as much of an engine in a small boat as you dare and see how fast it goes." Wood followed that philosophy throughout his racing career.

Miss Detroit III handily won the race. She also won the Gold Cup in 1919, and *Miss Detroit IV* won the cup in 1920 and 1921. Wood's domination of the race with his unlimited boats, and his almost unlimited money to build them, led to fewer challenges and less public interest. His powerful hydroplanes now reached 80 miles per hour. It was certain that they would win, so not many people wanted to race against them and few spectators cared to watch the races.

Change of Rules, 1922

The American Power Boat Association met in New York City in the winter of 1922 and changed the rules. It wanted to include normal boats that more people could race and banned hydroplanes. The association stringently limited the size of engines. The best boats permitted in the race had V-bottoms and might reach 40 miles per hour. The race was between less expensive, slower, and probably safer boats. The 1922 race brought in many more challengers.

Naturally Gar Wood was not happy. "I'm being robbed," he said. He attended the next Indianapolis 500 auto race, and it gave him an idea. There was no way that racing boats of the time could run for 500 miles at a stretch, but 150 miles was not beyond them. He was sitting beside Charles F. Chapman, chairman of the race committee of the American Power Boat Association, who had a large hand in the decision to change the Gold Cup rules. Wood verbally sparred with Chapman about that decision and proposed a 150-mile boat race. The 150-mile race would develop marine engines and boats as the Indianapolis 500 did for cars. Chapman was interested. A group returned to Detroit from Indianapolis, formed an organization to set up such a race, and named it the Yachtsmen's Association of America. Edsel Ford was the association chairman, and Chapman became chairman of the race committee. The Detroit Sweepstakes were established. Henry Ford contributed the first $5,000 toward the $25,000 purse to be divided among the winners.

Judson apparently saw no irony when he hired two Detroit boatbuilders, Martin and Jack Beebe, to build the boat he intended to race and bring the trophy back to where he thought it belonged. The builders produced a 28-foot hydroplane with a 12-cylinder, 600-horsepower Van Blerck engine, also made in Detroit. This boat, *Whip-O-Will, Jr.*, competed at the 1918 race against Wood's *Miss Detroit III*, a new boat powered by Wood's own marine conversion of a Curtiss airplane engine. One problem with race boats was that the more powerful their marine engines, the heavier those engines had to be. Wood realized that aircraft engines were designed to produce as much power from as

The Harmsworth Race, 1920

The most famous powerboat race in the world was the Harmsworth, the international contest, established in 1903 by Alfred Harmsworth, owner of the London *Daily Mail*. In 1920 in the first race held after World War I, Gar

Wood entered a boat, and so did his old opponent, A. L. Judson of the American Power Boat Association. Judson planned to race his Detroit-built *Whip-O-Will, Jr.*

One rule of the Harmsworth was that every part of a contesting boat had to be made in the country it represented. Wood used mahogany from Honduras because he believed that mahogany best stood up to the stresses that a racing hull encountered. There is no such thing as American mahogany, but he found a solution: Philippine mahogany. The Philippines at that time were under American control, and its exports were legal to use in the United States. He used Bosch carburetors and magnetos from Germany, so he collected every American magneto and carburetor made, studied them at length, rebuilt them, tested and retested them, and finally had what he wanted.

J. G. Vincent, engineering vice president of the Packard Motor Car Company, spent the war developing the Liberty airplane engine for the United States. A slim, pleasantly thoughtful man with a high forehead and retreating hair, he was still known by his wartime title of Colonel. Wood and Smith approached Colonel Vincent about engines for the race. Vincent told them of the work that had gone into developing the Liberty and advised them to adapt Liberties. The engines and parts were now available as postwar surplus, so Wood acquired four of them and a great many extra parts for the two boats he intended to build. The three contenders, one owned by Judson and two by Wood, were shipped to England as deck cargo aboard the steamer *Adriatic* in July 1920.

The races were on the Solent between the Isle of Wight and the English mainland. That stretch is known for rough weather, but Wood realized the race might occur on a quiet day. One boat was designed for smooth water and one for rough water. The smooth-water boat, *Miss America*, was only 26 feet long and powered by two Liberties for a total of 1,000 horsepower. The rough-water boat, *Miss Detroit V*, was 38 feet long—just two feet under the Harmsworth limit—and also had 1,000 horses. Wood drove the little *Miss America*, and his brother George drove *Miss Detroit V*.

Three English boats: *Sunbeam-Despujols*, *Maple Leaf V*, and *Maple Leaf VI*, opposed the Americans. *Maple Leaf V* had four engines, and *Maple Leaf VI* had two Rolls-Royce airplane engines. Sunbeam was powered by four 12-cylinder, 450-horsepower aviation engines. The Solent was quiet and smooth.

A Lloyds of London insurance agent had unwisely sold boat insurance to the American entrants. *Whip-O-Will, Jr.* caught fire during a prerace run and was completely destroyed. Judson was immediately paid the equivalent of $15,000, and thereafter, Lloyds refused to insure racing boats.

As requested by the insurance agent, Wood placed thin strips of tin over his spark plugs to protect them from spray. The thin strips interfered with the flow of air, and during the first heat of the race, the engines of *Miss Detroit V* overheated and blew out some of the plugs. She continued but fell back to a distant last place. Wood, in the little *Miss America*, had similar trouble, but the boat was so nimble he was able to cut closely around markers that the English boats had to circle widely. He came in first and left a cloud of smoke over the course. He and his mechanic were covered in soot. An astonished onlooker asked what he was using as fuel. Soft coal, Wood replied, but he'd use gasoline tomorrow.

The English boats were overpowered for their hulls and porpoised badly at speed. After Wood removed the offending strips of tin, his boats almost had the course to themselves in the following heats. On the unusually smooth water, *Miss America* won and *Miss Detroit V* came in second. The Harmsworth Trophy went to Detroit.

The Fisher–Allison Race, 1920

In 1920, while Wood was occupied with the Harmsworth, Carl G. Fisher, owner of the Indianapolis Speedway, ran the first of the Fisher-Allison races (Fisher provided $5,000 for the trophy; Allison gave the prizes) at Detroit. Fisher wanted a race that would start at the appointed time and not be delayed by weather that was unkind to hydroplanes, or by hydroplanes that struggled to get ready for the race. He was disgusted by the frequent breakdowns and occasional sinkings of the hydroplanes and disliked the fact that the engines of the fast boats often had to be rebuilt overnight between heats to keep them in the races. Fisher wanted to develop boats that could be used outside of racing. He established rules that his competition would start on time; the boats had to seat four people; the engines had to be enclosed, have self-starters, and workable reverse gears; and the race was to be run for an unbroken 150 miles.

The first Fisher-Allison race drew seven entries, including Fisher's *Miss Miami*, which ironically had mechanical troubles and did not start. The winner was *Rainbow*, driven by Harry Greening of Hamilton, Ontario, and built by Ditchburn, the best known of several builders on the Muskoka Lakes.

The Harmsworth Race, 1921

In 1921 there was an English challenge for the Harmsworth Trophy by Sir Mackay Edgar. Gar Wood had Smith build his boat, *Miss America II*. Smith didn't like the way that Wood wanted to have it built, but Wood persisted, and when it was completed he took it out and tested it. It wouldn't plane, so it went back to the shop. Smith altered the design of the step to what he thought was right, and the boat planed.

As the British challenger, *Maple Leaf IV*, was unloaded from a railcar, she was dropped about two feet and the hull was twisted out of line. She had been built of laminated wood under a British patent and the British mechanics went to work straightening the hull. The driver, Col. A. W. Tait, took the boat out on the river, gave a burst of speed, and a bearing in one of the engines promptly burned out. The British had no way to fashion a new bearing, and the race rules said that everything in each boat had to be manufactured in its country of origin by men of that nationality. At the request of the race committee, Wood waived that requirement and had his own men repair the damaged engine.

The race began two days later. Four Liberty aircraft engines, converted by Wood, powered his *Miss America II* and produced 2,000 horsepower. The British boat, *Maple Leaf IV*, had four Sunbeam engines that developed 1,800 horsepower. Wood also entered *Miss America I* in the race. Rough weather delayed the first heat, but Wood took *Miss America II* out for a trial run. She porpoised badly and he hurriedly took the boat in. The four Liberties had shaken the frame out of line, and the porpoising caused the wood at the heel of the step to peel away. The frame was straightened and the peeling was repaired by a brass strip placed across the step,

Rainbow III was considered the best racing boat of her day and competed for the 1923 Gold Cup at Detroit. It was designed by Hacker and built by Ditchburn on the Muskoka Lakes. She easily won two heats, but a cotter pin came loose during the third heat and she limped in to tie the race. The tie was broken by the arcane rules of the American Power Boat Association. The race went to the other boat and caused indignation in yachting circles. *Classic Boating*

The cockpit of *Rainbow III. Classic Boating*

held in place by countersunk rivets. Wood tried out the boat again, and it wouldn't plane. All day and night they worked on it, and Wood repeatedly took the boat out and found that none of the repairs made any difference. Eventually Wood's hull designer Napoleon Lisee saw that the brass strip protruded 1/16th of an inch and suggested that they take it off as a last resort. After that the boat planed beautifully.

The race itself was an anticlimax. On the second lap the laminate hull of the British challenger tore open. As a rescue boat towed her ashore, she caught fire. Gar won the race with his *Miss America II*.

The Fisher-Allison Race, 1921

In February 1921 the Fisher-Allison Race was held in Miami. Webb Jay of Chicago entered his new Hacker-designed and -built *Adieu*, a 32-footer powered by a 200-horsepower, six-cylinder Hall-Scott. Jay raced against *Rainbow*, a 32-footer powered by a six-cylinder Sterling. *Rainbow's* pilot was Harry Greening, the Canadian sportsman.

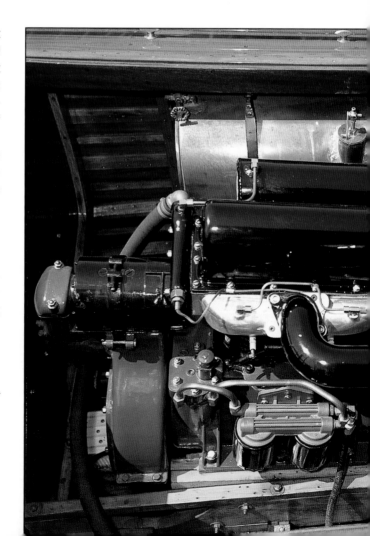

The six-cylinder, 200-horsepower Packard engine of *Rainbow III*, like other racing engines, ran on a mixture of 35 to 50 percent benzol with high-test gasoline. *Classic Boating*

The rudder assembly of *Rainbow III* incorporated many ideas of owner and driver Harry Greening. The rudder was of saw steel. It was flexible but didn't bend permanently under pressure. Ironically, a loose cotter pin lost the race. *Classic Boating*

Greening and *Rainbow* had won the previous year. A third contestant was *Orlo II*, a Hickman Sea Sled powered by two heavy Sterlings. *Adieu* was the dark horse.

In the first heat *Adieu* crossed the starting line first, followed by *Rainbow* and *Orlo II*. They kept in that order throughout the race and crossed the finish line in the same order. On the second day *Rainbow* struck a piece of floating wood, which damaged its propeller and seriously slowed the boat. *Adieu* stopped completely because of a bad spark plug, which was replaced. *Orlo* won that heat, followed by *Adieu* and *Rainbow*.

The third heat was held in the open sea. *Orlo* had engine trouble and did not start. Although Greening stayed in hot pursuit as the boats bumped harshly over the waves, *Adieu* crossed the finish line a few seconds ahead of *Rainbow*.

Smith and Wood Separate, 1922

In February 1922 Chris Smith and Gar Wood decided to separate their operations. The younger members of the Smith family, probably inspired by the nearby auto industry, wanted to build powerboats for more general sale. Wood owned controlling interest in the plant they shared, so the Smiths gambled their life savings to buy land in Algonac and build a new plant. Until it was built the Smiths and Wood shared the old shop and simultaneously produced commercial runabouts that were called Baby Gars and Chriscraft (no hyphen as in the later Chris-Craft). The new plant was completed at the end of 1922. Smith moved into the new building and Wood took over the older shop. The crew of workmen split and went to one or the other plant. Napoleon Lisee was a fine designer who had worked for Chris Smith since 1905, but Lisee had designed Wood's racing boats and went with Wood.

Wood took interest in the designs of his boats but concentrated on the engines. The hulls were largely designed by Lisee. For the next two years, Smith built the hulls of the Baby Gars for Wood. They then were sent to Wood's plant to have the engines installed. In 1921 Wood bought a railcar load of war-surplus Liberty aircraft engines and founded the Detroit Marine-Aero Engine Company to convert the engines for marine use. The new

Gar Wood heard some comments that his high-powered boats were not "gentlemen's runabouts." For the 1924 Fisher-Allison race at Buffalo he and his mechanic Orlin Johnson dressed in full evening dress as a humorous response. They drove *Baby Gar IV* and came in first. *Mystic Seaport, Rosenfeld Collection, Mystic, Connecticut*

company also bought up Fiat and other surplus aircraft engines to convert.

The Fisher-Allison Race, 1922

Colonel Vincent, the Packard engineer, had driven race cars and was interested in placing Packard engines in boats. In 1922 he bought a 32-foot Baby Gar, a boat that Smith was building for Wood. Vincent put a new Packard marine engine, derived from a wartime Liberty aircraft engine, into the boat that was named *Packard Baby Gar*. It and Wood's *Baby Gar III* ran in the 1922 Fisher-Allison Race at Hamilton, Ontario.

"Gar Wood," reported *Motor Boating*, "who up to this year had never entered a boat in the Fisher-Allison race, was called a burglar when he opened the hatches of his *Baby Gar III* and those nearby saw two six-cylinder [Fiat aircraft] motors of approximately 2,700 cubic inches piston displacement, installed and geared together through a gear box to a common propeller shaft.

Lady Helen won the 1924 Junior Gold Cup race. She was a Hacker-designed 21-footer powered by a Scripps Junior Gold Cup six. *Mystic Seaport, Rosenfeld Collection, Mystic, Connecticut*

"Those who previously had been most interested in the race had grown to believe it was their race…." Protests against the engines used in both Wood's and Vincent's boats were entered hours before the start of the race "by some of those owners who had not seen fit to enter their craft within the time allowed by the rules and in fact, in more than one case, have not as yet entered, strictly speaking."

Carl G. Fisher, who had established the race, was present. He was consulted and approved of the entries. Fisher in fact had been the one to suggest the formation of Wood's Marine-Aero Engine Company to convert airplane engines to boat engines. The boats were permitted to race, and Wood and Vincent came in first and second. Despite the founder's approval, the protesters were adamantly against the Detroit interlopers and the two protests were submitted to the American Power Boat Association for resolution. The magazine report pointed out wryly that all the breakdowns during the race were of engines whose eligibility had been approved.

The Association appointed Col. William Hayward to determine whether the protests were valid. Hayward was a U.S. District Attorney for New York. After considerable study, he announced that Vincent's Packard engine was a prototype not listed in any catalog and not generally available, as Fisher's deed of gift required. Therefore, that protest was upheld. Wood's engines, however, were produced by his Detroit Marine-Aero Engine Company, which had around six in stock and was ready to deliver them to any purchaser. They were within the provisions, but the American Power Boat Association had added its own additional rule that because of "a lack of experience as to the suitability" of airplane engines, no such engines could be used. Hayward noted that the wisdom of such a rule was beside the point. It excluded Wood's powerplant, and the protest had to be upheld.

The Gold Cup Races, 1922–1924

Back in Detroit, Wood offered Vincent a 26-foot hull to use as a Gold Cup racer under the new rules. Smith had finished it for Wood, and it became *Packard Chriscraft,* powered by half of a 12-cylinder Packard engine. The 1922 Gold Cup was run in early September, and Vincent won with *Packard Chriscraft;* Gar Wood and *Baby Gar Jr.* finished in seventh place. The Gold Cup Committee had tamed Gar Wood, but only in Gold Cup races, and they still had not managed to take the cup to the East.

In 1923 a new challenger, Harry Greening, of Hamilton, Ontario, entered the Gold Cup races. He had competed successfully in various other races with a suc-

cession of boats named *Rainbow* built by Ditchburn on the Muskoka Lakes.

Greening's boat in the 1923 race was *Rainbow III.* It was designed by John Hacker, built by Ditchburn, and powered by a 1M-618 Gold Cup Packard engine with 225 horsepower that used a mixture of 35 to 50 percent benzol mixed with high-octane gasoline. The boat was described by *Motor Boating* as "the neatest, finest, and best constructed craft" in the race. Greening easily won the first two heats. In the final heat he was well ahead of the others in the

In 1926, the Junior Gold Cup race was won by a Hacker design, *Lady Helen II.* Owner Aaron de Roy congratulates driver Dick Locke while John Hacker looks on. *Mystic Seaport, Rosenfeld Collection, Mystic, Connecticut.*

eighth lap when a cotter pin that secured the rudder broke. It took eight minutes to fix, and *Rainbow III* finished the heat in fourth place. The winner of the cup was the one who had the most points total for each heat—and fourth place only gave *Rainbow* five points in the third heat, for a total of 21. Vincent's *Packard Chriscraft,* driven by Caleb Bragg, came in second in each heat and had the same number of points as *Rainbow III.* In the instance of a tie, according to the American Power Boat Association rules, the cup would go to the boat that had the best total elapsed time in all heats, *Packard Chriscraft. Yachting* magazine said, "There is no doubt that *Rainbow III* was the best boat in the race…and it looks as if the system of scoring had something wrong with it."

In 1927 circus impresario John Ringling commissioned a 28-foot racer from Ditchburn. The company produced several boats of the same model. *Viking* was used as a fast boat by the Toronto Harbour Police. *Classic Boating*

Greening was back the following year with *Rainbow IV,* which was also built by Ditchburn and powered by the same engine as her predecessor. The Cup rules still barred hydroplanes but had been relaxed to permit lapstrake boats in the race, and *Rainbow IV* had the overlapping planks of a lapstrake boat. Her bottom, however, was planked crosswise (instead of the usual fore-and-aft planking), and in effect, gave her a number of small hydroplane steps. As seasoned a competitor as Greening, he must have known that this construction might be challenged, and it was. The challenge was entered before the race, but the race committee decided to toss the hot potato to the American Power Boat Association for their decision as to what constituted a hydroplane, and meanwhile the race went ahead. *Rainbow IV*

Miss America VII. Chris-Craft Collection, Mariners' Museum, Newport News, Virginia

Barbara ("Betty") Carstairs, a British challenger for the Harmsworth Trophy in 1928, 1929, and 1930, was one of the few women in boat racing. *Chris-Craft Collection, Mariners' Museum, Newport News, Virginia*

was not as clearly victorious as *Rainbow III* had been, but she was first on points and was proclaimed the winner at the Gold Cup banquet. In due course, the American Power Boat Association upheld the challenge.

Greening took *Rainbow IV* back to the Muskoka Lakes and broke all records by running for 24 hours over 1,218.88 miles at an average speed of 50.78 miles per hour. He essentially won the Gold Cup twice, but he never received the cup. Greening was apparently either satisfied or disgusted with that contest because he never entered it again.

The Detroit Sweepstakes, 1923

The first 150-mile Detroit Sweepstakes race was held on the Detroit River in 1923. Fifteen boats competed, and eight finished. Two of them, the

Estelle IV, a British challenger for the 1929 Harmsworth Trophy, dropped out with engine trouble and was towed ashore by a Chris-Craft tender. *Chris-Craft Collection, Mariners' Museum, Newport News, Virginia*

Teddy and the *Bruin*, belonged to Wood. He had a pair of teddy bears that he always carried as mascots, and one rode in each boat. It was the only time they were separated. Smith had built three boats—*Packard Chriscraft II*, *Packard Chriscraft III*, and *Miss Packard*—for Colonel Vincent.

Bruin, driven by Phil Wood, began to fall apart and dropped out early in the race. George Wood, another brother, drove *Teddy* and persevered. Vincent drove *Packard Chriscraft II* and led the pack for 32 laps until the distributor of his boat malfunctioned, cut out half of her 12 cylinders, and slowed her down. *Teddy* passed her, and on the 43rd lap, *Teddy*'s hatch covers blew off. She was in the lead by a short distance and her crew did not want to stop to pick them up. The rules of the race stated the hatch covers had to be on when the boats were running. Gar Wood was standing with the judges—where he didn't belong—and one of the judges pointed out that they had to flag in the boat to pick up the hatch covers. Wood objected strenuously and managed to cow the judges. On the next-to-last lap, Wood, who by that time had moved to his own pit, had someone take the covers off *Bruin*, picked up the flag, and signaled in *Teddy*. The crew took up the hatch covers, put them in place, and came in first.

Vincent lodged a protest against Wood, and when Wood heard of it he was outraged. Wood asked Chris Smith if he'd heard that Vincent was going to protest. "If he doesn't," Smith said, "he should." Wood became so angry that he threatened to get an injunction to prevent distribution of the prize money. That evening at the postrace banquet at the Detroit Yacht Club, after Wood introduced his brother George and his mechanic, Orlin Johnson, he said, "These men have raced the finest and fastest boats in history. In spite of what they had against them, they turned out the winning boat. No one can take that from them—*no one*." He said no more, and all present, who had expected a more violent performance, breathed a sigh of relief.

Restless, a 26-foot Chris-Craft racing runabout from 1930, was powered by an 825-ci Chris-Craft engine and competed through 1948. *Classic Boating*

The next day the race committee met and decided that the rules had not been sufficiently explicit that hatch covers had to be on for the whole race. Therefore, Wood's boat won. The committee evidently was under pressure to avoid a confrontation with the explosive star, and the following day they resigned as a body. Vincent noted in his diary, "My protest was not allowed for some reason."

The Fisher-Allison Race, 1924

Wood did have a sense of humor. In 1924 the Fisher-Allison race, from which both Wood and Vincent had been disqualified in 1922, was held at the Buffalo Launch Club. After diplomatic haggling—the attitude of the boating press and the implied attitude of Colonel Hayward toward the 1922 race certainly strengthened Wood's position—Gar Wood's modified aircraft engines were permitted, although he had to limit their displacement. He used a 12-cylinder Liberty for this race, and only two other boats were entered. During the negotiations, there were scornful comments that his boats were not "gentlemen's runabouts." The remarks probably also echoed feelings of East versus Midwest, and old money versus new money. Wood's humor responded. He and his mechanic dressed in white-tie evening clothes and wore them during the race. They won, and when they came up to the judge's stand in spotless full dress, Gar doffed his top hat to the judges. The hat had been equipped with a chinstrap to hold it on during the race.

Smaller Racing Classes

John L. Hacker designed a number of racing boats in the smaller classes. Before World War I, he produced a class of runabouts useful for one-design racing—the 151s. In the early 1920s, people began to put auto engines in the runabouts. The engine that was used most often was the "Fronty-Ford," a converted Model T engine.

In 1924 and 1926, two of Hacker's other boats, *Lady Helen* and *Lady Helen II,* won the Junior Gold Cup—races for smaller craft run under Gold Cup rules. *Lady Helen* was powered by a Scripps "Junior Gold Cup" six-cylinder engine, and *Lady Helen II* had a Miller engine. In 1926 Hacker launched the 151-cubic-inch Pelican class of very small racers. This class became dominated by boats of Hacker's design named *Spitfire,* owned by Buffalo millionaire James H. Rand Jr. Rand's boats were powered by Fronty engines.

In an early race of the Pelican class, held at Buffalo in August 1926, *Spitfire IV* won the first heat but crashed after it crossed the finish line. Rand was fished out, dried out, and supervised the transfer of the engine from the wrecked boat into another hull, *Spitfire V,* that night. The *Spitfire V* won the race.

The following year Mrs. Rand needed a boat to enter in the race for the Duke of York's Trophy in England. *Spitfire V* was given a supercharged eight-cylinder Miller engine, was renamed *Little Spitfire,* and was shipped off to England where she handily won the trophy. Then *Little Spitfire* returned to the United States and entered an international race staged by the *Detroit News* in September 1927. It won in a field that consisted of boats from Canada, England, Germany, and one other from the United States.

The Detroit Sweepstakes, 1924–1927

The 150-mile Detroit Sweepstakes lasted through 1927. Wood won the second in *Miss Detroit VII;* Vincent won the third in *Packard Chriscraft II.* The fourth was won by *Rowdy,* built by the Purdys (who by that time had moved from Michigan to Long Island) and owned by the Carl Fisher who had established the Fisher-Allison race; and the fifth was won by *Miss Syndicate,* a boat built by a syndicate formed by the main owner, Horace Dodge Jr. of the auto family. The race was no longer drawing many contestants, and it was not scheduled thereafter.

The Harmsworth Races, 1925 and 1926

Wood returned to the Harmsworth race in 1925 to meet a challenge for the trophy from Henri Esdres of France. Esdres had built the *Excelsior-France* that was powered by two 16-cylinder engines. Wood accepted the challenge and immediately set to work on two new racers, *Miss America III* and *Miss America IV.* After they were built, the *Excelsior-France* burned. It was too late for the French to build another boat for this race, which was canceled.

Esdres built a boat for the following year. Wood didn't build anything until he learned that the French boat had been packed up and was on its way to the United States. He built *Miss America V* in less than 15 days.

The *Excelsior-France II* was put into the water on the day of the race, and it listed. The officials postponed the race until the boat could be righted, but then the challenger could not operate its starter and start its engines without bottles of compressed air, which the French had not brought with them and that were not readily available in Detroit. The boat was not able to come out on the water the day the race was scheduled, so it was again postponed.

Wood agreed to waive the rules and had his mechanics work on the French boat while others scoured Detroit for the right kind of compressed air bottles for the boat. None were found and nothing worked. On the next race day, Wood's men towed the boat around the river until the engines started. The race began, and the challenger's engines died. Wood's boats completed the course.

The Harmsworth Race, 1928

In 1928 Marion Barbara Carstairs challenged for the Harmsworth. She was an English heiress who had commissioned the constructions of race boats and had won races in Europe. Her mother, Evelyn Estelle Bostwick, had been an American (the boats were all named *Estelle*), and her father, Joseph F. Carstairs, was an Englishman. Marion was going to school in the United States when World War I occurred. She was 16 and went back to Europe to join an organization called The American Ambulance, attached to the French army. After the war she became interested in motorboat racing. Her mascot was Lord Tod Wadley, a small male doll dressed to miniature Saville Row perfection.

Wood accepted the challenge and built *Miss America VI,* a 50-foot hydroplane powered by two newly designed Packard aircraft engines of 1,000 horsepower each. Wood opened up the engines on an early trial run. The boat nosed down and the lightly built hull flew apart. Wood suddenly found himself underwater, fought his way to the wreckage-littered surface, and looked for Orlin Johnson, his mechanic of many races. Johnson bobbed to the surface

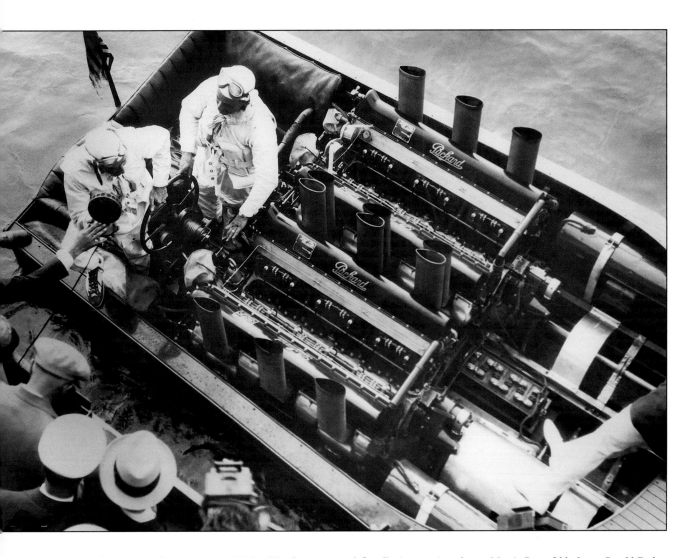

The engines of *Miss America IX*. Gar Wood, at extreme left, talks into a microphone. *Morris Rosenfeld photo, Gerald Farber*

and had suffered a gash on his throat from the accident. Jay Smith, president of Chris Smith & Sons Boat Company, observed the trial run from a nearby boat. He fished Johnson out of the water, took him ashore, and rendered first aid. Another boat picked up Wood. Johnson was unconscious for more than an hour, and when he opened his eyes he said, "Guess we'll have to build another boat."

Johnson was sent to a hospital in Detroit. Wood was in bed for a day and called his boatbuilders, led by Napoleon Lisee, together at his home. They planned a new, stronger boat to replace *Miss America VI*, but the only engines of that model that Packard had built thus far had been on the destroyed boat. Wood sent divers to the bottom of the river to search for them. Five days after the accident the divers located the engines, and a Packard truck stood by to rush them back to the factory where Packard experts waited to rebuild them, but all that the

experts had to do was to take the engines apart, clean them, and reassemble them.

A new boat, *Miss America VII*, complete with reinstalled engines, was ready in two weeks. Johnson, the battered mechanic with his broken jaw still in a cast, was lifted into the cockpit, and Wood drove. On the second lap of the race at the west turn, Carstairs' *Estelle II* nosed down, flipped over, and threw out her and Harris, her mechanic, at some speed. Carstairs floated unhurt in her life jacket and called to the rescue boat to get Harris, who was hurt. He was taken to a hospital where he was treated for two broken ribs and a spinal injury.

The Championship of North America, 1928
A race for the Championship of North America was held at the Detroit Regatta after the 1928 Harmsworth contest. This was the only time that such a race took

place. Perhaps it was scheduled because the Gold Cup race was canceled that year.

Greening's entry was designed and built by Ditchburn on the Muskoka Lakes. The 35-foot runabout was said to seat eleven people comfortably. She was a two-step hydroplane equipped with two Gar Wood Liberty engines. She was named *Rainbow VII* and painted black with an emerald bottom.

During each heat Greening carried at least seven people in his boat. He had only one competitor, who sank on the second lap, during the first heat. Additional boats had been called in by the time of the second heat. Three other racers all fell well behind *Rainbow VII,* which averaged almost 60 miles per hour. One of the three boats did not finish. The two that survived entered the third heat, and in addition, Gar Wood put in *Miss America V* and *Miss America VII.* Wood's boats took the first two places in that heat, and Greening's took third place. Because *Rainbow VII* had led the first two heats, she was declared the winner and took home the Championship of North America.

Greening took *Rainbow VII* back to the Muskoka Lakes. The next year he used her in an endurance test on Lake Rosseau, with an official timer from the American Power Boat Association to keep the records. In 12 hours, including the time for refueling and changing crews (Greening alternated as driver), the boat averaged 60.325 miles per hour. This was a new record that beat the one he set in 1925 with *Rainbow IV.* Setting the record capped Greening's active racing career, but he continued to officiate at races.

The engines of *Miss England II* were located behind the cockpit. *Dossin Great Lakes Museum, Detroit*

Miss England II led *Miss America IX* in the first heat of the 1931 Harmsworth race. *Dossin Great Lakes Museum, Detroit*

The Harmsworth Races, 1929 and 1930

In 1929 Barbara Carstairs returned with a heavier boat. *Estelle IV* weighed 4 tons. Wood had *Miss America VII* and the new *Miss America VIII*. George Wood and mechanic Captain Woolson manned *VII*, and Gar Wood and Orlin Johnson manned *VIII*.

On the third lap of the race, the manifold of the port engine on *Estelle IV* came loose and fire streamed from the cylinders. Carstairs was afraid the boat would burn up, so she turned off the engine and drifted out of the race.

Before she went home, Carstairs and her crew, at Wood's suggestion, studied the lines of the American boats and took notes. Her new boat that was built in England had two 900-horsepower V-12 Napier Lion engines. She returned in 1930 with *Estelle IV* and the new *Estelle V.* Wood had *Miss America V, Miss America VII,* and the new *Miss America IX.*

Carstairs' *Estelle V,* driven by the English racer Bert Hawker, quickly passed *Miss America IX,* driven by Wood. The English boat's oil line broke shortly afterward and

sprayed the crew with hot oil that blinded them. Hawker, unable to see, lost control, and the boat rushed off course. Hawker regained control and managed to get back on course and pursue Wood. As Hawker passed the judges' stand at the beginning of the second lap, his gas tank ruptured and the engines caught fire. The crew subdued the flames, but then the gas tank was empty.

Barbara Carstairs finished the heat in *Estelle IV.* She gave the boat to Hawker and told him to drive it in the remaining heats until it broke up if that was necessary to win. But as with the other boat, the rivets holding the gas tank together tore out before the heat was completed, the gas tank emptied itself, and the boat stopped.

The Venice Regatta, 1929

Immediately after the 1929 Harmsworth, Wood shipped *Miss America V* and *Miss America VII* to the Venice Regatta, because Henry Segrave, the rising English speed champion, had invited him.

Segrave had twice been to Florida to set new land speed records at Daytona. The first time, in 1927, Wood invited him to his winter home at Indian River and gave him a ride in *Miss America V.* Segrave returned in 1929 and set another land speed record, and he also brought a boat with him. Wood looked it over, pointed out problems with the propeller and rudder, obtained some new propellers of the type he thought was the best, and had his mechanics install a new propeller and rudder on Segrave's boat. They had an impromptu race between *Miss America VII* and *Miss England.* Wood's boat had been lying in Florida's saltwater too long and her steering cable was eaten away. The cable broke at the first turn. Segrave went back to England determined to get support to build a Harmsworth challenger.

When *Miss America VII* was shipped off to Venice, her hull had been strained during the Harmsworth race, and it was not repaired in the rush to get to the race. After they arrived in Venice, Phil Wood and Orlin Johnson looked over the weakened boat and decided they were committed to race and that it was up to them to crew it. Prince Carlo Ruspoli would drive *V,* with Vance Smith as mechanic.

When the race began, the crews of the two Wood boats were somehow late across the starting line. *V* crossed it in a rush. Immediately *VII* passed at high speed, leaped into the air, and threw out Wood and Johnson. The boat curved into the shore and crashed.

Smith turned down his engines and Ruspoli steered beside Johnson, who seemed dead as he floated in the water. Smith dragged Johnson aboard and began to administer artificial respiration while Ruspoli headed for the dock. A doctor pronounced Johnson dead, but Smith put Johnson in one of the fast runabouts that always stood by at races in case of emergencies and rushed him to a hospital, working on him as they went. Just as they reached the hospital landing, Johnson gasped and breathed again. He was alive but had a fractured skull. Phil Wood was picked up by another boat and taken to the hospital. He was considerably bruised but not seriously hurt.

The engines of *Miss America X* from 1932. Gar Wood constantly honed these engines to extract more power. *Dossin Great Lakes Museum, Detroit*

Miss America X, Gar Wood's ultimate racing machine, at speed. *Dossin Great Lakes Museum, Detroit.*

The Disputed Harmsworth Race, 1931

Lord Wakefield, in response to Segrave's request, challenged Wood for the Harmsworth. He had *Miss England II* built for the race. She weighed 7 tons and was powered by two new aircraft engines of 2,000 horsepower each. The boat was tested on Lake Windermere in England, with Henry Segrave behind the wheel and two mechanics on board. Segrave commented before the test that it was Friday the 13th. On the second pass over a measured mile, Segrave opened up the engines. The boat rushed across the lake, made a sudden turn, leaped out of the water, and threw the crew overboard. Segrave and one of the mechanics died.

After the accident, Wakefield said that he would never support racing again, but as time passed and other owners asked for the special engines from the old boat, he changed his mind. He rebuilt *Miss England II* and challenged Wood for a 1931 race. Kaye Don would drive *Miss England II*.

Wood was the first man to travel over 100 miles per hour on water, but Don had reached slightly more than 103 miles per hour in his rebuilt boat at a trial in Buenos Aires. Wood had superchargers built for the engines of *Miss America IX* and for those of *Miss America VIII* to match Don's boat.

The day of the first heat was calm and the water was smooth. Kaye Don was first across the starting line, Gar Wood (with a recovered Johnson as mechanic) was a boat length behind in *Miss America IX*, and George Wood was a short distance behind that in *Miss America VIII*. Gar followed so close behind Don that the pounding of *Miss America IX* on the wake of *Miss England II* began to strain the structure of the American boat, breaking several planks and many frames, which caused the boat to handle strangely. Gar dropped back slightly. The first heat ended with Gar 45 seconds behind Don; George Wood was 20 seconds farther behind. *Miss England II* clearly seemed to be the fastest boat.

They took *Miss America IX* to the boathouse at Wood's home nearby and worked all night to repair her structure. All seemed well until they started to fill the fuel tanks and discovered that one was cracked. A hole had to be cut in the deck, the tank had to be removed and soldered, and then the procedure reversed. Wood asked for a 30- to 45-minute delay—a courtesy that he had often given opponents. Don asked if he had a second boat, and Wood did. If Wood agreed to use only the second boat, Don would agree to a postponement. That would take the best American boat out of the contest, which was exactly what Wood tried to prevent. Wood refused, and the committee denied the delay.

It is easy to understand Don's feelings. He had come a long way and was ready to race at the appointed time. The race was held in Wood's territory, yet Wood's boat had not been well prepared and wasn't ready. Don's boat seemed obviously superior in the first heat, and now Wood appeared to stall.

Wood hastily finished the repairs and ran wide open to the starting line in order to get there on time. He passed Don, who also was starting toward the line. Don immediately speeded up to gain the lead. Both boats crossed the starting line ahead of the gun and were disqualified. *Miss America VIII* was behind the boats and properly crossed the line. Wood and Don continued as though they were unaware of their mistake. Wood was in the lead and Don tried hard to pass him.

The English boat became hard to handle and skidded several times. Don tried to straighten out the boat, and crossed Wood's wake, and *Miss England II* flipped over. No one was seriously injured, but feelings were greatly hurt. *Miss America VIII* came up on the accident, paused doubtfully, was flagged on again, and was the only boat to finish the race legally. There was a third heat the following day where *VIII* ran around the course and crossed the finish line, but the racing commission later ruled "no match." Only two countries raced, and one had been disqualified in two of the three heats. Therefore, the heat was eliminated, so essentially there had been no race.

There were immediate accusations that Wood had intentionally lured Don to cross the line early to disqualify both Don and himself because he thought *Miss America VIII* could not beat the English boat and that he had planned for his slower boat to go on and win. These accusations quickly reached the press on both sides of the Atlantic. *Miss England II* obviously had been fastest in the first heat, and Don was a skilled driver. Theorists saw a one-man conspiracy, and those who witnessed Don's stiff-necked behavior before the race thought Wood was out for revenge. Although the theories do not withstand examination (Neal, in *Packards at Speed,* gives a careful analysis of time, speed, and geography, and concludes that Wood could not have tricked Don even if he had wanted to), they did poison relations between American and British racers for some time. They are occasionally brought out again to this day.

The Harmsworth Race, 1932

Lee Barrett was sent to England on a diplomatic mission to confer with English race officials. He took the chart for a new course laid out on Lake St. Clair by the superintendent of

lighthouses. It was a course that was much better from the racers' viewpoint than the older, narrow one that did not give boats room to maneuver, so that one boat had to pass another through the heaviest part of its wake. The new plan did not, however, permit crowds (over 200,000 spectators had watched the last race) to line the shores and sustain the sport. The English bodies that governed the Harmsworth matches gave approval. Lord Wakefield had the noted builders John I. Thornycroft Ltd. start work on another racer, *Miss England III*. This boat was very similar to the pattern of Wood's boats. When the new boat was completed, Kaye Don took her to Loch Lomond and set a new water speed record of 119.81 miles per hour.

Wood had to have a new, faster boat. He decided that he would build only one. He wrote to a friend that he thought it was the most fair to enter only one, which perhaps reflected the Kaye Don imbroglio. The English engines were more powerful than American ones, and Wood seemed to be at an impasse. He decided to take the four Packard engines (two each) out of *Miss America VIII* and *Miss America IX* and use them to power *Miss America X.*

Miss England III. Gerald Farber

Horace Dodge, a member of the Detroit Yacht Club, drove *Delphine V* in the 1932 Gold Cup race at Lake Montauk, New York. The Duesenberg engine failed and the boat was towed from the course. Dodge stands on deck while the mechanic studies the problem. *Gerald Farber*

Packard reworked the engines, and each six-cylinder bank of the V-12 engine was fitted with a new type of supercharger. Wood used a fuel mixture of one-third alcohol, one-third benzol, and one-third gasoline to lower the engine temperature. Each engine produced 1,600 horsepower after it was adjusted and tuned. The boat itself was 38 feet, 9 inches long and weighed 14,000 pounds.

Miss England III had two supercharged V-12 Rolls-Royce aviation engines that were recently developed for the British Air Ministry. Each engine produced 2,200 horsepower. The design of Wood's engines was eight years old, and they had been constructed four years earlier. The English boat was 35 feet long and weighed 10,500 pounds.

Nine days before the 1932 race, one of Wood's engines broke a connecting rod during a trial run. These engines had never before been tuned to produce so much power or to put such heavy loads on their parts. Wood had the four engines taken out of the boat and sent them to Packard to have all rods replaced with stronger ones. The engines were back in the boat in eight days.

Miss England III arrived two weeks in advance and was housed in a Grosse Point boathouse that was one of the most luxurious in the United States. The boathouse was about 100 yards from the starting line, and the boat was never brought out before the race.

In the 1932 Gold Cup race, the *Delphine IV* gave Dodge a rare victory. The boat represented Detroit; Dodge owned the boat, and William Horn was the winning driver. *Gerald Farber*

The first race was supposed to begin at 6:30 A.M., but Lake St. Clair was choppy and the start was delayed until 7:00. The two boats crossed the line slightly after the gun, with Wood five seconds behind Don. Wood was in second place until the end of the fourth lap when he passed Don. Don's engines seemed to misfire and became increasingly worse until his boat completely stopped.

The next race was scheduled for three days later, which gave Don two days to repair his engines. The repairs were supposedly completed, but the boat was never taken out of the boathouse to be tested.

In the second race, the two boats both crossed the line a few seconds after the starting gun. Both drivers opened their throttles, and Wood gradually crept ahead. The engines in *Miss England III* began to smoke and shoot flames. By the second lap, one engine had stopped. The other engine expired at the end of the second lap. After the race, Don's explanation of what had happened did not fit the symptoms seen when the engines failed. There was much speculation, including the thought that he was protecting the reputation of Rolls-Royce and the Air Ministry.

After the race, on September 20, 1932, Wood ran *Miss America X* over a measured course on the St. Clair River and set a new speed record of 124.91 miles per

El Legarto was an older boat of Hacker's design. George Reis, her owner and driver, won the Gold Cup in 1933, 1934, and 1935. In the 1933 race (shown) are *El Legarto* and *Delphine VII*, driven by Delphine Dodge Baker, Horace's sister and the first woman to compete for the Gold Cup. *Gerald Farber.*

hour. Later that year, Lord Wakefield announced that he was retiring from racing.

The Gold Cup, 1929–1935

Interest in the Gold Cup was waning, so the American Power Boat Association changed the rules for the 1928 Cup. Planing hulls were again allowed, although the engine rule (maximum size of 625 cubic inches) remained the same. The 1928 races were canceled because of heavy traffic on the Hudson River, where the races were going to be held, but they continued in 1929. Both Wood and Vincent were 48 years old and no longer in the prime of athletic condition needed to withstand the pounding that a race boat gave its crew. Wood's hair was turning a shade that led sportswriters to call him the Silver Fox. Wood, however, was still willing to undertake the Harmsworth competitions, and six years later when a reporter asked him how it felt to travel at two miles a minute in *Miss America X,* he had a one-word answer: "Uncomfortable."

Future Gold Cup rosters listed new names, and the most prevalent was Horace E. Dodge, heir to the auto fortune. The boats he raced usually were built in his own boat-building plant, but he seldom seemed to win. As a result, it appeared that the Gold Cup would never return to Detroit, and Dodge was largely dismissed as a dabbler. He proved them wrong in 1932 when his *Delphine IV,* driven by William M. Horn and representing the Detroit Yacht Club, finally won the Gold Cup at Lake Montauk, New York. This victory prompted someone at the Detroit Yacht Club to telegraph him, "COME HOME, ALL IS FORGIVEN."

In 1933 the races were held in Detroit on the day before the next Harmsworth. *Delphine IV,* owned by Dodge and driven by Horn, was the defender. Four other *Delphines,* all owned by members of the Dodge family, were also entered in the race. *Delphine IX,* driven by Dodge himself, came in

fourth. *Delphine VII,* driven by Delphine D. Baker, Dodge's sister, finished third. A very dark horse, *El Legarto,* a racer designed and built by John L. Hacker, won the contest and set new records for lap and heat speed.

El Legarto was built in the Hacker plant in 1922. It was first named *Miss Mary* and was driven unsuccessfully by the first owner. The boat languished until George Reis bought it in 1925. He brought it up to the changed Gold Cup standards by installing a Packard engine with over 300 horsepower and shingling the bottom with 5/8-inch steps. She went on to win the 1934 and 1935 Gold Cup races at Lake George, New York. The famous boat can be seen in the Adirondack Museum.

The Gold Cup, 1936–1939

The Gold Cuppers used engine designs that dated back to World War I. They were tuned to give much more than their designed horsepower, but the result was much more stress on their parts. As a result, breakdowns were common. The 1936 Gold Cup race was a fiasco. The only competent boat and driver involved were Horace Dodge's *Impshi* driven by Kaye Don. They won the race and brought the cup back to Detroit.

By 1937 the Gold Cup races seemed lackluster, but Detroit produced a quarter of a million spectators. The host city also produced *Notre Dame,* powered by a 24-cylinder supercharged Duesenberg engine and driven by Clell Perry, her designer and builder. This was the first Gold Cup race to have European entries. Ten boats competed in the race, including *Alagi,* powered by a supercharged Isotta-Fraschini airplane-type engine and driven by her Italian owner, Count Theo Rossi di Montelera. She was supposedly the world's fastest boat aside from Harmsworth Trophy craft. The race developed into a duel between *Notre Dame* and *Alagi.* The water was rough for hydroplane racing, and all the others except the little *Hotsy Totsy III,* driven by Bill Horn, fell out. *Alagi* won a single heat and proved hard to control in rough water. *Notre Dame* screamed a high-pitched song of speed from

A Depression-era Special Race Boat from Chris-Craft. The 26-foot *Jay-Dee II* was produced in 1934. With a light hull and specially tuned Chris-Craft V-8, it was a constant winner. *Classic Boating*

her Duesenberg and drove steadily ahead to become the winner. *Hotsy Totsy III* bravely came in a distant third.

By the late 1930s some of the smaller racing classes no longer required their boats to carry mechanics during races. Italian and French boats began to enter American Gold Cup races during this time. The European boats provided no room in their cockpits for a second person. In 1937 the Gold Cup contest board voted to allow one-person boats to participate if they carried 150 pounds of extra ballast, which was supposedly the average weight of a mechanic. Mechanics were no longer necessary to attend the engines but had become navigators to provide a second pair of eyes to spot markers and floating logs and observe the other boats, and a second pair of hands to operate stopwatches. In the following years, riding mechanics gradually disappeared.

In 1938 the Italian *Alagi,* racing under the colors of the Miss Detroit Power Boat Association, won the Gold Cup against feeble opposition. *Alagi* did not compete in 1939 because her owner could not leave Italy with the approaching war. *My Sin,* an American boat of a new form, carried the 1939 trophy off to the Atlantic Seaboard.

My Sin was a three-point hydroplane. She rode on sponsons attached to each side of her bow and on a single point at the stern. The bottom of the hull was concave. At speed, air rushed between the sponsons and beneath the hull to create lift. There was little contact between the sponsons or hull and the water. The partly submerged propeller was the basic point of stability. As a result, the boat could reach high speeds. More conservative mariners objected that these craft were airplanes and suggested that unlimited racing should be divided into airborne and waterborne classes, but the whole evolution of fast hydroplanes had been driven by one idea: having as little contact between hull and water as possible. The airborne racers were the logical culmination, and the suggestion for two classes was never adopted.

The Harmsworth Race, 1933

The day after the 1933 Gold Cup, there was another Harmsworth race. Three-point boats still were not involved. The course was to be on the St. Clair River off Marine City, north of Algonac. In 1933 the challenger was Hubert Scott-Paine, an Englishman who was based at Chris Smith's boat plant. He brought a number of mechanics and a supply of spare parts. His *Miss Britain III* had an aluminum hull that was 24 feet, 6 inches long. The boat was powered by a single 1,375-horsepower Napier engine and weighed 3,360 pounds as opposed to *Miss America X's* 15,000. Wood used his Algonac plant as his base.

The location of the race was away from the city, so there were fewer spectators. After a delay because of rough water, the two boats crossed the line at about the same time. At the end of the race, *Miss America X* was 90 seconds ahead of *Miss Britain III*. The second race began the following Monday, which was Labor Day. Scott-Paine crossed the starting line a few seconds ahead of Wood, but Wood soon passed him. Scott-Paine, however, had put a new engine in the boat since the last race, and his boat seemed to move more quickly. At the end of the race Wood was just 22 seconds ahead.

There was not another Harmsworth challenge until 1949, due in part to World War II.

The 225-Cubic-Inch Class

The 225s were launched by John Hacker. He drew up the rules for the class that the American Power Boat Association accepted. The boats were going to be a limited-cost class. Initially, a limit was imposed on the price. For instance, engines could cost no more than $700. By 1935 the 225 Class had become so popular that *Motor Boating* magazine hailed it as "America's Greatest Race Class." That year 38 225s had been built and more were under construction. They were popular with racers and the public, and contrasted vigorously with the stodgy Gold Cup boats of the day.

The Racing Wilsons

On the Muskoka Lakes, near Georgian Bay, Tom Greavette turned out a series of racing boats for Harold Wilson. Wilson won several titles with them, and the first was in a Hacker-designed 225 boat at Toronto in the early 1930s.

Early in Wilson's racing career, his mechanic was always his fiancée, Lorna Reid. It was an unusual courtship, but what better way for two people to learn if they were compatible. They were both students at the University of Toronto. As they traveled to races, there were minor complications to make sure that Miss Reid was always properly chaperoned. When designing their boats, Hacker insisted on having two cockpits; a smaller one for Reid behind the larger one for Wilson. Hacker believed the difference in their weights would unbalance the boat if they sat side by side.

The Last Prewar Gold Cup Boats

Wilson graduated from the 225s to the Gold Cup Class in 1936. A new *Miss Canada II,* designed by Hacker and crewed by Wilson and Reid, entered the Gold Cup race at Lake George, New York, in 1936. She succumbed to engine problems and—in company with seven other competitors—did not start. Wilson's boat had a new and recalcitrant Miller engine, but most boats had engines whose old, overstressed designs constantly failed. Only

Jay-Dee III, a 19-foot Chris-Craft Special Race Boat from 1935, was the first of a model built for a European group racing on the Rivera. This boat stayed in the United States, and it set a new world record for its class of 45.330 miles per hour in the 1935 President's Cup Regatta. *Classic Boating*

John Hacker originated the highly successful 225-cubic-inch class. *Little Miss Canada IV*, one of his international champions, was built by Greavette in 1935. Hacker put the driver and his mechanic and fiancée in separate cockpits so that their different weights would not spoil the craft's balance. *Muskoka Lakes Museum*

two boats raced, and one fell out during the race. The winner was *Impshi*, owned by Horace Dodge and driven by Kaye Don. Wilson's boat only lasted through the first heat at the 1937 Detroit Gold Cup race.

Soon after the 1937 race, Wilson and Reid were married. In the 1938 Gold Cup race held at Detroit, Wilson ran a new boat. The Greavette-built *Miss Canada III* was designed by Doug Van Patten and equipped with a Merlin engine made by Packard under license. When the boat started, the mechanic had to stand in the engine compartment and pour a Coke bottle full of 150-octane fuel into the eye of the supercharger. As the boat surged ahead, the mechanic had to close and lock the hatches and crawl back to the cockpit over the whaleback deck of the boat. Lorna performed this duty while

the boat was being prepared for the race, but she and her husband had a serious discussion of what might happen to their children if both parents were hurt during a race. Lorna retired as a mechanic before this race, but she was still involved in all the other aspects of the racing organization. In the 1938 race, *Miss Canada III* came in third. Five other boats did not finish. *Miss Canada III* also competed in the 1939 Gold Cup race at Detroit and again came in third.

Wilson took the Greavette boat to the 1939 President's Cup race in Washington and won. Franklin Delano Roosevelt presented the cup, which is kept by the winner for a year. When a bystander objected that the deed of gift prevented it from being taken outside U.S. boundaries, Roosevelt replied, "My dear young man, you had better realize that Canada is not a foreign country; it is a brother country. Take it home, Mr. Wilson."

After the race, Canada had just entered World War II and Canadian racing halted for the duration of the war. U.S. defense preparations soon halted racing there as well. The last prewar Gold Cup race was held at Red Bank, New Jersey, in 1941. Only one boat came, and it was declared the winner.

IA 4308 AM

CHAPTER 3
RUNABOUTS

Runabouts

In 1904 boatbuilder Fitz Hunt raced his motorboat *Terrible* against the fast 269-foot-long steamer *Toronto* between Alexandria Bay and Clayton on the upper St. Lawrence River. Both contestants traveled about 20 miles per hour, and *Terrible* won by a small margin. At a time when greater size was still thought to mean greater speed, the laws of physics seemed to have crumbled. The gasoline-engined boat had arrived.

The first Gold Cup racers were called "auto-boats." As gasoline-driven boats became more accepted, personal craft developed that were called "runabouts." Runabout was an automotive term equivalent to what "sports cars" means today. Apparently the term was first used for boats on the upper St. Lawrence in the Thousand Islands region,

just east of Lake Ontario. The Thousand Islands were a summer resort area for well-to-do people—people who could afford to buy attractive boats—and the sheltered waters were an ideal place for small, nimble, and speedy craft to evolve.

The name runabout was first applied to almost any motorboat that could move and maneuver quickly and smoothly. The name shifted to more specifically represent a boat with a powerful engine (for that time period) under a forward deck. In extreme models, the deck ran more than half the length of the boat. Runabouts often were early racers and remained close cousins to racers in later years. Some runabouts continued to race in contests in which the boats were limited by type or power.

A 1931 28-foot Chris-Craft Model 216 Custom Runabout. *Classic Boating*

Powered Skiffs

Another cousin to the runabout, on the more sedate side of the family, is the powered skiff. A variety of small engines were put into the famous St. Lawrence rowing skiffs. The result was the "skiff-putt." It earned its nickname from the "putt-putt" noise the engine made.

The Muskoka Lakes, just east of Georgian Bay, was another area where well-to-do people spent summers. Rocky terrain surrounds the Muskokas and, in the early days, few roads existed, so water transportation was essential. W. J. Johnston Jr., a skiff builder in the area, developed a propeller and driveshaft that protruded from the bottom of the boat, just aft of midships, that could be retracted into the craft if the boat was beached or lifted onto a pier. The propeller and driveshaft were fitted with a protective skeg that automatically raised them if they met an obstacle underwater.

Johnston patented the device, obtained financial backing, and formed the Disappearing Propeller Boat Company in 1916. Its trademark was Dis-Pro, and the common name for both company and boat became Dispro. Soon the fond owners and skeptical bystanders called the boats by the initials D.P., pronounced Dippy—the name that remains in use today. The boats the company built were slightly larger versions of the original skiffs. They were nicely varnished, still clinker built and double ended, and 16-1/2 feet long.

Some of Johnston's boats found their way to the upper St. Lawrence River. One description of the skiff-putts says that there were disappearing propeller boats known as Dispros among them. The skiff-putts had various types of engines, but all were primitive and notorious for being difficult to start and operate.

The skiff-putts and the Dippies provided modest motor-driven transportation for some years while the runabouts developed in their own way. The skiffs of the St. Lawrence evolved into St. Lawrence River double-ended fishing boats, 26-footers with larger and more reliable engines, often taken from old cars. The Dispro builders eventually went out of business in the face of competition from outboard motorboats.

Semi-displacement Hulls

As power increased in runabouts, designers evolved the semi-displacement boats by widening hulls at the stern to keep them from squatting. The sterns often were shallower than the bows of the same hulls, although the propeller and rudder added to the depth of water the boat drew. Eventually most powerboats had transoms at the stern to tie the broad width and shallow depth together.

Sylvan Jr. was an early 24-foot Thousand Islands runabout. It was built in 1914 by Hutchinson for Jean Chapman, a summer resident in the region, who drives the boat. *Bonnie W. Mark*

As models developed, fine lines forward cut into the water, then widened to the nearly flat bottom aft to produce a semi-displacement round bottom or V-bottom hull. These hulls planed at faster speeds. The round bottom was a development of the standard boat shape, and the V-bottom combined the sharp bow of the knife-on-edge displacement boat with the flat bottoms of traditional craft such as sharpies and dories. The new hull designs became popular with the designers of small, fast boats. The V-bottom boat can be identified by a strong angle at the turn of the bilge, where the side meets the bottom. The edge made by that angle is called the chine.

The Gidleyford

In the late 1800s, boatbuilder Henry Gidley set up shop in the Georgian Bay town of Penetanguishene (a Native American word usually shortened to Penetang). By the early 1900s, he built boats for the Canadian government and the Hudson's Bay Company, in addition to his local customers. The Russian government also ordered five icebreaking boats from him. By the 1920s, the Gidley boat shop was well established and built everything from large cruisers (up to 110 feet long) to semi-displacement runabouts, the boats for which Gidley was best known.

Show Girl, a 27-foot 1921 Hutchinson, was once owned by stage and screen actress Irene Purcell. *Classic Boating*

In 1922 the Ford Motor Company of Canada and Gidley joined forces to build the Gidleyford, a small V-bottom boat with a sharp bow, powered by a Ford Model T engine. The boat had a Model T steering wheel and windshield, and the folding top used on Ford's open cars. The Gidleyford was made out of cedar planking on oak frames and available either varnished or painted. Few creations emphasized the close tie between powered boats and automobiles as the Gidleyford.

These boats went into Ford car showrooms in Canada. The marine versions of the Model T engines were also sold separately. The boats were priced at $1,400, and the engines were $300 in 1924. The success of the boats apparently was modest. Not many seem to have been built and apparently none has survived.

Another Gidley boat, the *Kittyhawk* (no connection with the Hacker racing boats of the same name), was used by Orville Wright to reach his cottage on Lambert Island in Georgian Bay. An open 32-foot V-bottom with a long forward deck, she was a semi-displacement boat that could plane at speed. Wright bought her in 1929 and later added a closed sedan top. The boat survived and has been restored.

During the late 1930s Gidley sold out to Grew, another Canadian company that still exists today.

Marine Engine Builders

Builders of marine engines developed in the evolving motor city of Detroit and in other places as well.

The Kahlenberg brothers' machine shop in Two Rivers, Wisconsin, built and installed a one-cylinder, two-stroke engine for the owner of a 35-foot Mackinaw fishing boat in 1898. They had their own patented fuel-injection system by 1914. Soon they built the favorite engine for commercial fishermen on the Great Lakes and produced and exported engines for commercial and yachting use throughout the world.

In 1903 Charles A. Criqui and a group of businessmen bought the faltering Sterling Engine Company in Buffalo. At that time, the company produced one-, two-, and three-cylinder two-cycle engines. It produced some four-cycle engines by 1907. In 1910 it advertised engines that ranged from two to eight cylinders, and it may have been the first company to produce an eight-cylinder marine engine. Sterlings powered most Gold Cup boats of the time. The company was well established by World War I, and it produced a large number of marine engines for the war.

In the late 1890s the Michigan Yacht & Power Company in Detroit built the first boat to navigate the Yukon River under power. The company was headed by O. J.

A Disappearing Propeller Company boat, usually called a Dispro or DP (pronounced *Dippy*), around 1920 in the Muskoka region. The powered skiff was a cousin to the early runabouts. *Muskoka Lakes Museum*

Mulford, a professional advertising man who carried the accounts of Ford, Packard, and other companies. In 1905 the company became the Gray Marine Motor Company with Mulford as full-time president and two Grays—sons of a millionaire who helped underwrite Ford—as vice president and secretary/treasurer. The company soon offered eight engine sizes that ranged from 1-1/2 horsepower to 24 horsepower. Under Mulford's guidance, Gray advertised widely and successfully sold engines domestically and abroad.

William E. Scripps was a well-to-do Detroit yachtsman and publisher of the *Detroit News.* Immersed in the Detroit environment, he wondered if internal combustion engines could be applied to boats. As a hobby he designed and developed a four-cylinder, four-stroke, 25-horsepower

engine and put it in a boat. It was successful and his friends pressured him for similar engines. He built a factory and began to make engines in 1906. Scripps Motor Company changed direction somewhat in 1910 and produced heavier engines for a wider market. In 1915 it introduced an enclosed flywheel and the electric starter as standard equipment.

Joe Van Blerck, a Dutch immigrant, is given credit for designing the engine that Ford used in his Model T. In 1909 Van Blerck started a small engine-building shop in Detroit. It was a one-man operation, and his products became well known for their quality. He concentrated on marine engines that were mainly custom designed, so spare parts had to be made to order. Around 1910 he was joined by Charles E.

Pioneer aviator Orville Wright used the *Kittyhawk* in the 1920s to reach his summer cottage on a Georgian Bay island. Gidley built the *Kittyhawk* and had earlier joined with Ford of Canada to produce a smaller model called the Gidleyford. The *Kittyhawk* has been restored. *G. Johnstone Collection, Huronia Museum*

The 1922 Chris-Craft runabout *Godfather*, powered by a Curtis OX-5 Chris-Craft V-8 conversion, follows the pattern of Hacker's original Bear Cats. It has a single cockpit forward and a large area for wicker chairs aft of the engine. *Classic Boating*

Page, a Cleveland businessman, who put up the money for a new factory in Monroe, Michigan, a short distance from Detroit. Page took over the administration, an aspect Van Blerck had never liked. Van Blerck continued to build engines and progressed to make standard models that were considerably lighter than the competitors' models. His engines were in many of the early racing boats.

In 1910 the Kermath Manufacturing Company ran a general machine shop in Detroit. It surveyed the marine-engine field and decided to build a 12-horsepower motor that would satisfactorily propel 80 percent of all the motorboats being

number of machine shops and boatbuilders converted other auto and airplane engines for marine use. In time, Chris-Craft produced its own engines.

John L. Hacker

The best-remembered designer of runabouts (and other boats) is John L. Hacker, the oldest in a family of 11 children, who grew up in Detroit. He supposedly built a boat in a year during his teens. He attended night school and took correspondence courses to learn engineering and boat design while he was a bookkeeper for his father's ice and coal business. In 1903 he built *Au Revoir*, a 32-foot boat with a 55-horsepower engine that was hailed by *Motor Boat* as "the fastest boat of her size and power in this country."

Hacker's business history was complicated by bad health. He established the Hacker Boat Company when he bought the Detroit Launch & Power Company in 1908. In 1911 his racing boat *Kitty Hawk* (not the Canadian boat of the same name) was said to be the first 50-mile-per-hour boat in the United States, but that same year, his doctor told him to take a vacation probably to relieve stress. He sold the company, and in 1912 he worked for the Van Blerck Engine Company before going back into boat design. In 1915 he joined the Albany Boat Company at Watervliet, New York. The following year he had another breakdown and spent some time in a sanitarium before he returned to Detroit and refounded the Hacker Boat Company. Hacker was one of the first designer-builders to use the V-bottom hull for his boats.

In addition to building boats to sell, Hacker designed boats for other builders. Some of his boats in 1918 were runabouts designed and built for the Belle Isle Boat & Engine Company in Detroit, which were sold as "Belle Isle Bear Cats." They were probably the first stock runabouts that had controls in cockpits forward of the engines. They were powered by 100- to 150-horsepower Hall-Scotts. A large open space was aft of the engines. It wasn't a true cockpit yet and was usually filled with wicker chairs. The Belle Isle boats were highly successful and established Hacker as a leading designer.

Under his own name, Hacker designed and built the first stock runabouts to reach a speed of 40 miles per hour, fitted with six-cylinder Hall-Scotts. They were two-cockpit boats, but like the pure racers of the day they were controlled from the aft cockpit. Edsel Ford purchased one in 1920.

Hacker Moves to Mount Clemens

In 1921 Hacker set up a branch operation in nearby Mount Clemens, Michigan, and two years later he moved his headquarters to a new plant there. He marketed his

made at that time. It built a four-cylinder, four-cycle engine of 12 horsepower. The engine was ahead of its time, appeared to be too complicated, and did not attract buyers at first. John B. Farr, the newly appointed sales manager, went from town to town and builder to builder to promote the new engine. Sales gradually grew, and the company then produced a 20-horsepower engine they advertised internationally. Success at home and abroad followed quickly, and Kermath became an established name.

Soon several makers of automobiles, such as Chrysler, Dodge, and Packard, began to turn out marine engines. A

Rebel, a 1924 Hacker 33-foot special, was the second of two built. The first boat went to Henry Ford. These boats were among the earliest to have the double cockpit and windshield forward, and one of the earliest to have barrel-backs. Hacker streamlined some of his custom boats but never used barrel-backs or bows in his stock boats. *Classic Boating*

boats under the general name Hackercraft and called his runabouts Dolphins. C. P. McCready financed the plant and installed his son, S. Dudley McCready, as secretary of the Hacker Boat Company in 1925. The McCreadys provided a firm business structure that supported Hacker's artistry.

Hacker was company president but did not always fit easily into this new business arrangement. In 1925 S. Dudley McCready wrote an admonishing letter to him and pointed out a violation of the contract between him and the McCreadys. Hacker was having a Gold Cup boat of his design built by his old friends in the Belle Isle Boat Company because he had "certain personal financial difficulties." The letter, in effect, said that they would let him do it this once "with the distinct understanding that the Belle Isle Boat Company's name shall in no way be connected with this boat...and that the Hacker Boat Company

shall receive the benefit of any success it may have, but don't do it again." The company agreement had always permitted Hacker to have cruisers of his own design built elsewhere. It is not clear what the personal financial difficulties were, but Hacker is generally remembered as a genius of design yet a hopeless businessman.

Smith and Wood

In 1922 Chris Smith & Sons Boat Company ended its racing connection with Gar Wood, moved to a new plant it established, and adopted the name "Chris-Craft" for its new stock runabouts. Smith continued to build the hulls of Wood's Baby Gar 33-footers, which were then sent to Wood's shop where the 450-horsepower aircraft engines converted by Wood were installed. These powerful brutes were probably the first stock boats to go faster than 50 miles per hour. They were first used in 1921, mainly for use in local races, but after the change in Gold Cup rules in 1922, the interest in Chris-Crafts became much wider. They usually had a small forward driving cockpit located nearly amidships. Most of the space behind the forward cockpit was filled with a huge engine, followed by a tiny aft cockpit, which the mechanic occupied during a race.

Many of the Baby Gars were sold to eager millionaire sportsmen, but Wood also began to produce a more typical runabout design for general use in some of the 33-footers. In 1927 he entered the market with 26- and 28-foot boats. The 26-footer was called Baby Gar Jr. He built and sold 102 of them, but he abruptly discontinued the Jr. the following year apparently because it was barely profitable. Initially, Kermaths powered his smaller boats, but Chrysler Imperial engines replaced them. The Chrysler engines provided speeds of 32 to 35 miles per hour. In 1929 he built 202 of the 28-foot Baby Gars.

Dodge

In 1924 the Dodge family of automotive fame established a Detroit boat-building plant. They appointed a rising young designer, George F. Crouch, as vice president, and produced runabouts they called Water Cars. The Horace E. Dodge Boat Works bought surplus Curtiss airplane engines from the government and converted them to use in the boats. The company offered two models of 22-footers and two models of 26-footers in 1926. The faster boats in each size had Dodge-Curtiss engines that propelled them to over 30 miles per hour; the slower ones had Dodge marine engines.

The business was established for Horace Dodge's son, Horace Jr., who was widely known through the tabloids

thanks to his five marriages. Horace Jr. had no interest in auto manufacturing, but he drove racing boats. His mother, Anna Dilman, who controlled the Dodge millions, set up the boat-building company and named Horace Jr. president. The plant's automotive background made it a simple production-line operation, probably the first one used in boat building, and the boats were well made. If the company had had better management, in time it might have rivaled Chris-Craft. The plant also built Dodge's racing boats and advertised that it would build racers to order, although not many people took advantage of that service. By 1927 it produced 22-, 26-, and 30-foot standard-design Watercars.

The Runabout as a Commercial Product

Hacker, Smith, and Wood developed the runabout as a commercial product. All of them did custom work on occasion, although Smith probably did less than the others. The runabouts provided basic sales for all three companies. Most of Wood's production boats, like Chris-Craft's, had double planking on their bottoms with a layer of canvas between. Hacker varied the construction according to the type of boat, but his stock runabouts had double bottoms with a center layer of canvas. One curiosity modern restorers have found on Hacker stock boats is that the inside layer, which was laid diagonally, meets at the keel and forms an arrowhead shape that points forward. In Wood and Chris-Craft boats, the inner planking arrowhead points aft. Both designs seem to work equally well.

The Classic Runabout

The runabout evolved in several ways. Some boats still had cockpits and controls aft. Some had forward cockpits but were operated from the aft cockpit. The boats that had controls in front cockpits were the forerunners of what we now consider the classic model. The forward cockpit in front of the engine hatches was small and had no windshield, while a large open space behind the engine that usually held several wicker chairs could scarcely be called a cockpit. Hacker's Belle Isle Bear Cats were probably the first stock boats with this arrangement.

In 1924 John Hacker introduced what probably were the first stock runabouts that had a double cockpit forward, protected by a windshield, and a small cockpit behind the engine hatches. This design is now known as the classic

Hacker's 1924 24-foot Dolphin was probably the first stock boat with a forward double cockpit and windshield. A 125-horsepower Scripps engine drove the boat up to 33 miles per hour. *Tom Flood*

When Bill MacKerer, a designer for Chris-Craft, had a falling out with the company, he moved for a time to the Rochester Boat Company. One result was this handsome 28-foot Rochester runabout from 1926. *Classic Boating*

runabout. It was a 24-footer driven by a 125-horsepower Scripps engine. The same year, he also built two custom 33-footers with the same cockpit arrangement. At that time, Dodge was just beginning to build its stock boats, which only had aft cockpits. Chris-Craft stock boats still copied the Bear Cats and had controls in a small forward cockpit and the large open space aft. It changed to the classic style late in 1925. Wood's 33-footers were still built by the Smiths of Chris-Craft and mainly used for racing. They were usually controlled from aft cockpits, but around this time Wood began to offer them for more general use with the classic arrangement.

Hacker's boats led the group in bottom design, styling, and construction. They were called the Steinways of boats, and it is generally considered that he was ahead of everyone else in most aspects of runabout evolution. Many Chris-Craft, Gar Wood, and other models looked like boats that Hacker had designed earlier. A common joke was that the competing builders bought one of each stock

boat that Hacker produced so they could copy it. His runabouts were made with a sheer line that lowered slightly as it went toward the bow. It allowed better visibility when the boats were moving at speeds that caused the bow to rise. Under Hacker's artistic hand, the boats looked extremely graceful. Other designers, even to the present day, have copied the slim reverse curve, although sometimes heavy hands have produced ugly boats.

Hackercraft boats were also known for the level smoothness of their ride, and the design of their bottoms was copied as much as their lines. Around 1929 Hacker changed from concave V-bottoms to convex V-bottoms, which curved slightly outward rather than inward. The new design made the boats ride more easily in heavy weather. Perhaps because this change happened at the start of the Great Depression, most of the other stock boats were still built with concave bottoms.

All three men were absorbed in boats, but that is where the similarity ended. Smith worked from half models

that he carved, and once said he wasn't interested in calcu-
lations. His chief designer, Napoleon Lisee, said he didn't
need blueprints—he began by laying out his boats full-size
on the floor. Wood was more interested in engines than in
boats and depended on Lisee to design his racing boats.
When Smith and Wood separated, Lisee went with Wood.
Hacker, on the other hand, was the engineer-designer
who worked out everything on his drawing board. He was
the artist whose slim curved boats were fast-moving
works of sculpture.

Smith's operation was a family one. His sons, Jay,
Bernard, and Owen, all worked in the business, and his
daughter, Catherine, kept the books for a while. In 1927 Jay
became president and Chris was chairman of the board. All
major decisions were family ones, and apparently all were
made without difficulty.

Mass Production

The Smiths at Chris-Craft were unable to turn out as
many boats as they could sell. In 1922 their first production
model was a V-bottom 26-footer. Its cockpit was surrounded
by a coaming but didn't have a windshield. A surplus
wartime Curtiss aircraft engine the company converted for
marine use powered the boat.

In 1922 Smith hired William MacKerer. Smith's leading designer, Napoleon Lisee, was well established in the
company and an expert traditional designer and builder
who scorned the drawing board and used teams of craftsmen to make his boats. Lisee clashed with MacKerer, an
experienced man who had worked for Hacker, among
many other companies. MacKerer was a trained naval architect who was devising a mass-production system that
would eliminate skilled craftsmen. Everything MacKerer

Early Dodge boats followed the cockpit-aft pattern. *Dazzle*, a 1925 22-foot, 5-inch Watercar—as Dodge runabouts were
called—was powered by a 30-horsepower Dodge engine. *Classic Boating*

Harvey Firestone and family take Thomas Edison for a jaunt in the Firestones' *Cadet*. The 1927 22-foot Chris-Craft, powered by a Chrysler six, was built by a largely automated assembly line. *Chris-Craft Collection, Mariners' Museum, Newport News, Virginia*

did went against the grain with Lisee. MacKerer was known for his volatile temper, and the confrontation between him and Lisee must have been explosive. MacKerer left the company.

MacKerer worked at the Rochester Boat Works for a while. Although the company was mainly known for its cruisers, MacKerer also designed runabouts for it. When Wood and Smith separated their businesses, Wood made sure Lisee went with him because he depended on Lisee to produce his racing boats. The Smiths now needed MacKerer more than ever. MacKerer returned in 1926 and set up their first full assembly line. That year Chris-Craft advertised 11 models in four lengths that ranged from 22 to 30 feet. MacKerer established careful records of production

costs, and his factory methods allowed the company to price its boats less than most of its competitors.

In June 1927 *Motor Boating* published an article on "The New Cadet," a recently introduced Chris-Craft model.

Not long ago it took a good man the best part of the day to turn out one keel; now the stick of wood for the keel passes through a machine and the finished keel comes out in a very few minutes, rabbetted, cut to length, shaped and planed in one operation. The same is true of the other major parts of the boat construction, ribs, frames, engine bed, floors, planking, transom, interior trim, bulkhead parts, seats, deck beams, and deck planking, in fact everything is machine made and finished. A keel set up has the frames and ribs in place and is ready for the planking within hardly more than an hour. The double planking is put on in short order by a gang of men who do no other work in the boat's construction. The lumber, screws, hardware, fittings, etc., are delivered to the men in the construction gangs in the proper amounts for each job, completely cut to size, and finished so that there will be no delay.

This system sped up construction and let Chris-Craft counter one of the problems of wooden boat building: the waste of material. In the hand construction of boats, each piece of wood is shaped and trimmed to fit in place, and a fraction of the wood is lost each time. This was not the case in the Smith plant. As wood was precut, every piece trimmed away was destined for use somewhere else. The smallest bits were turned into the wooden plugs driven in to fill countersunk screw holes. The final trash, much of it recovered from the shop floor by an industrial-size vacuum cleaner, was burned in the factory furnaces. Unlike some of the other builders, the Smiths and MacKerer kept careful records of the costs of building their boats and maintained tight control.

A story that suggests the Smiths' control of materials tells of Chris Smith's encounter with a fireman going off duty from the boiler room. The fireman's overalls were liberally coated with coal dust. Smith supposedly said, "Go back and brush off that coal. It belongs to me."

In the past, new boats had largely been sold to nautical-minded people who had previously owned boats. In 1927 Chris-Craft announced that it had completely reversed the pattern so that 90 percent of its sales were to those who had never owned boats before.

Chris-Craft's production and distribution already followed the automotive practice. It also offered new models each year, although these often were last year's models with some slight rearrangement. The final move toward the similarity with automobiles was that Chris-Crafts were offered for sale on installment credit. Chris-Craft introduced its own V-8 engine, designed by Jay Smith, in 1928. Chris-Craft resembled the Detroit automakers even more.

Dodge

The Dodge fortune was controlled by Anna Dilman, the mother of Horace Dodge Jr. Late in 1928, a boom year for most concerns, she announced that the Detroit boat-building plant would close because it was losing money. Dilman quickly changed her mind, but the Dodge boat-building

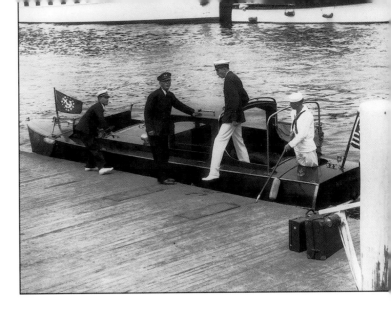

In 1927 Chris-Craft offered a 26-foot Special Yacht Tender that remained available throughout the 1930s. It was used on at least 30 large yachts. Vincent Astor steps ashore from his tender. *Chris-Craft Collection, Mariners' Museum, Newport News, Virginia*

operation was in trouble. Horace, the supposed manager, was living in England with his new second wife, and George Crouch, designer and vice president, had left.

To lure Horace back to the United States, his mother promised him millions of dollars to fulfill his boat-building fantasy: a new superplant. She bought a hundred-acre piece of land in Newport News, Virginia, and they planned and built the factory.

Horace wrote a self-promoting article that appeared in the February 1930 issue of *Motor Boating,* called "Mass

Ditchburn, on the Muskoka Lakes, delivered this 38-foot mahogany lifesaving boat to the Toronto Police in 1929. The boat was a one-step hydroplane with a six-cylinder, 200-horsepower Sterling. It was designed by Hacker and could travel at 36 miles per hour. *Toronto Port Authority Archives*

Wampum, a 1930 Gar Wood 33-footer. *Classic Boating*

Production for Boats." Regarding mass production, he said, "Naval architects, executives, bankers, and other students of the progress of motorboating have been predicting this for many years." He announced that boat building must be put "on the same building and merchandising plane as that of automobiles" and strongly implied that his new factory would be the first to do so. This must have left the people at Chris-Craft wondering what they had been doing for the past several years.

The cardinal event for Dodge was the operation's move to Virginia in 1931. The move was forecast in his 1930 article, and the name of the company was updated. It was now "The Horace E. Dodge Boat & Plane Corporation," which had "general offices in New York, and the largest and most completely equipped motorboat factory in the world now under construction on a hundred-acre waterfront site at Newport News, Virginia." This was

Baby Zackaroo, a rare 1931 Dee Wite 17-footer, was powered by a 50-horsepower Lodge four-cylinder engine. Dee Wite, founded in 1929, did not survive the Great Depression. *Classic Boating*

the first large boatbuilder to move away from the Great Lakes. The Virginia city was said to be a transportation center that would help the distribution of the boats. What may have gone unsaid was that it did not have the difficult labor climate of Detroit.

In his article Dodge wrote grandly, "We feel that after twenty-five years of arduous existence, the American motorboat industry is now about to come on the long delayed prosperity that its leaders have dreamed of for many years." He said he was going to travel the world—to the Orient and Australia—and sell the boats made in his fine new factory.

The Great Depression

Fate was waiting for a man as pleased with himself as Dodge. His company made the move to Newport News, and then the Great Depression hit. The concern did inaugurate a 16-foot runabout and a 19-foot utility, called the Dodge All-purpose, that helped to keep the company alive for a while. Horace dropped in from time to time, but as an absentee manager, he had not been able to keep a company profitable during the boom years of the 1920s. He now had little chance to survive the Depression. What may have been the company's last gasp was a 1935 advertisement for a 26-foot cruiser (shown only as a drawing and perhaps never built), a small sailboat, and the 16-foot runabout. After continuing losses, the plant was closed. It may have built a few custom racing boats, but it did nothing else until World War II, when it took on war construction. At the end of the war, a few fragments of the company were moved back to Detroit to build Horace's racers, but there were no more Dodge runabouts.

Gar Wood

Gar Wood found that the old Algonac plant he had originally bought from the Smiths of Chris-Craft was too small, so he moved much of his operation to a new, larger factory in Marysville, Michigan, in 1930. The construction of his racing boats and of some custom orders remained at Algonac. The Great Depression had come, and he built only 32 boats in 1931. In 1933 the factory, which was designed to build 1,200 boats a year, turned out 64. The Gar Wood factory survived the Depression largely because its owner had enough money to keep it afloat.

Chris-Craft

Chris-Craft was slow to feel the Great Depression. In 1929 it sold nearly 1,000 boats. Most of them were sold in the United States but some were shipped to 30 other countries. The company offered 24 models in 1930 and began

Leo III, a 1930 Chris-Craft 26-footer. *Classic Boating*

further expansion. It happily drove into 1931 and offered 37 models. That year, it lost nearly $200,000 of preinflation money. In the next few years the company survived only through the tenacity of the Smith family and some very adroit financial high-wire balancing.

Hacker

The Hacker Boat Company employed about 150 people by 1928. Its boats were sometimes considered lightly built; they had lighter frames than Chris-Craft, for example, but more of them. However, at the beginning of World War II, the U.S. Navy compared boats and noted that Hackercraft were heavier than comparable boats from Gar Wood, but Hackercraft pounded less and used less fuel at speed. John L. Hacker's boats had a flatter, smoother ride than others, and the quality of their construction was considered the finest. In June 1930 the company delivered 90 boats, which was probably its peak effort.

In 1930 John L. Hacker and his son John A. Hacker had a brief connection with the Century Boat Company. At that time, Century built outboard and light inboard boats, and the company had just been reorganized. The Hackers may have invested some money in it. John A. was its president for a short time; John L. was its designer. Within a year, the company began to produce inboard runabouts that competed in a general way with Hackercraft, and the Hackers withdrew. Century went bankrupt soon afterward because of the Depression.

The Depression also struck hard at the Hacker company. Boat sales fell alarmingly in 1931, even though no one argued with the statement in the 1931–32 Hackercraft catalog that "every fast runabout on the market today pays tribute by constantly imitating Hackercraft features. In the Hacker technique is noted a fine blending of artistic lines with staunch construction and supreme efficiency in running lines." A bright spot in 1932 was the completion and

An early 17-foot hardtop Lyman Utility. At the depths of the Depression, Lyman built small, lapstrake, white-painted inboards called utilities, which originated the term. They sold well at a time when glossy, varnished runabouts did not. *Tom Koroknay*

launch of Hacker's custom-designed and -built 40-foot, torpedo-shaped runabout *Lockpat II*. It was built for an owner who planned to use her to commute between his home in the country and Detroit. She was fitted with a 650-horsepower Packard engine, but the sales of stock boats, which provided the bread and butter for the company, nearly came to a standstill that year.

Disaster lay ahead for Hacker. The reasons are not clear. Perhaps the McCreadys had simply come to the end

of their patience with their artistic but unbusinesslike designer and decided to foreclose. On December 31, 1934, the board accepted the surrender to the company of all shares of stock held by John L. Hacker, including those in his son's name, "in payment of his indebtedness to the company." The younger McCready became president and his wife became the secretary of the company. The names Hacker Boat Company and Hackercraft now belonged to the McCreadys.

The Senior Hacker kept what must have been a lonely office at the plant for a time, although he quickly found another office in Detroit. He again agreed not to design boats for builders that would compete with those of the Hacker Boat Company, and to design boats for the company, although it no longer gave him credit in its advertising. Hacker designed cruisers and commuters and sold standardized "Hackerform" plans for about $30 (in Depression money). He scraped out a poor living, lost his home in the Detroit suburb of St. Clair Shores in 1940, and moved to a small house in Detroit.

Dee Wite

The Depression was not a good time for the established companies, and it was a really bad time for new companies. In the bright, optimistic days of early 1929, the Dwight Lumber Company of Detroit began to produce Dee Wite runabouts. The boats sold so well that in 1930, Dee Wite expanded its plant to include a new monorail that carried the unfinished hulls through the varnishing and drying process. The boats were well built and some models were ultrastreamlined, the then-fashionable shape; but all runabout sales were fading, and Dee Wite had gone out of business by 1935.

The Lapstrake Boats of Lyman

Lyman was one company that built boats for the nautical-minded and not for the recent converts lured from autos. The company, located in Sandusky, Ohio, on the open sweep of Lake Erie, was somewhat removed from the automotive influence of Detroit. Lyman provided a boat in the seagoing tradition. Peter Spectre wrote in the May/June 1988 issue of *WoodenBoat*, "When I was a kid, growing up in Massachusetts.... Anybody who had an appreciation for powerboats of any kind had a Lyman, or knew someone who had a Lyman, or was saving up his money to buy a Lyman.... Lymans were real boats, nothing at all like those cushioned and chromed dandymobiles held together with 75 layers of French-polished spar varnish."

The Lyman boatworks had moved to Sandusky from Cleveland in 1928. It had been in Cleveland since 1875 and had built everything from rowboats to sailing yachts. In 1924 it decided to focus on stock model outboard boats—outboard motors were being produced in the thousands by Johnson, Evinrude, Elto, and smaller manufacturers—and after it moved to Sandusky, it built an 11-footer and a 15-footer, both with lapstrake planking, usually of cypress on steam-bent oak frames.

Thanks to the Depression, by 1930 there was little demand for outboard boats, which had been popular with less affluent people who now had to save their money for shelter and food. Bill Lyman, manager of the company and the founder's son, made a surprising decision. He moved upmarket and introduced a 17-foot inboard boat, also with lapstrake planking, constructed of the same woods, and painted white except for varnished transom, trim, and small forward deck. It was an open boat that could be used for many purposes. He called it the Lyman Utility Inboard. The name "utility" may not have been glamorous, but it was certainly apt. The boat sold well. It was more usable and flexible than the runabout. There was room in it to move around and the engine was under an easily accessible box in the middle of the boat. It was a round-bottom boat but was also a semi-displacement design and could travel at a good speed. The utility was in the tradition of some of the earlier pleasure boats, before such features as cockpits, engines under hatches, mahogany planking, and varnish. It sold to people who had not been hit too hard by the Depression but who did not want conspicuous, fast, varnished boats at a time when many people had trouble buying food. Lyman gradually expanded the line. In 1931 he produced a semi-custom lapstrake 23-footer with a Kermath engine that drove the boat more than 25 miles per hour. By the late 1930s when other boatbuilders had to cut back their lines, the company offered 24 models that were mainly powered by Gray engines.

Boats of the Muskoka Lakes

"Once upon a time, not so very long ago, the better sort of pleasure boat was built, not manufactured," said William M. Gray in the preface to his book on the launches of the Muskoka Lakes—the interconnected Lake Muskoka, Lake Joseph, and Lake Rosseau. That sort of building was done, more recently than in almost any other place, in the Muskoka area, which lies in Canada just east of Georgian Bay. The Muskoka Lakes are surrounded by rocky terrain and had few roads around them; they soon became a center of boat building.

Muskoka Design and Workmanship

In his book, Gray points out that the most obvious difference between American boats and the Canadian boats was the understatement of the latter. (This is, to some degree, still a basic difference between the inhabitants of the United States and those of Canada.) Instead of having the maker's name painted in large letters on the outside of the craft, it was shown discreetly on a small metal plate fixed to the dash panel. Outside identification, if it existed at all, was by the design of the cove line along the side of the hull. The name of the boat was in metal letters near the bow or on

The 1922 Ditchburn mahogany-hulled, 38-foot *Dolly Durkin*. With her 275-horsepower Sterling, she could travel at 36 miles per hour. *Muskoka Lakes Museum*

raced internationally. Ditchburn still made the round-bottom displacement boats for less adventurous owners, and it also offered four V-bottom models. In 1926 the Canadian government ordered six high-speed patrol boats to regulate rumrunners on the Canadian Atlantic Coast. The basic design for these craft led to the development of Ditchburn's Viking model, which was a faster boat for other customers.

the boards that shielded the port and starboard running lights. The name wasn't on the transom. Canadian boats had less bright metal work.

Fashion on the Muskokas lagged behind, but often followed, the U.S. boats. At first, metal fittings were polished brass. They changed to aluminum, then nickel-plated brass or bronze, and finally chrome plate. American boats generally looked more rakish and copied automotive fashions, and a few years later, Muskoka builders might follow these fashions. After World War II when most American builders forgot streamlining, Greavette still produced streamliners. On the other hand, some American boats looked crudely finished beside the custom creations of Muskoka artisans.

Most engines used in the Muskoka boats came from Detroit, although Buchanan engines powered some of the smaller ones. In the nearby town of Orillia, Fred Buchanan began a machine shop that gradually developed into a factory. In the late 1920s, he built engines including the Buchanan Firefly engine that was used for an early model built by the Port Carling Boat Works.

Ditchburn

Ditchburn was incorporated in 1907 by Herb and Alf Ditchburn and Tom Greavette. By 1910 the company sold 26- to 30-foot displacement boats. Wood-framed windshields appeared around 1912. The engines were closed in under forward deck hatches, and metal stems glistened. In 1919 Harry Greening commissioned Ditchburn to build the first of a series of racing boats named *Rainbow* that he

Minett and Minett-Shields

H. C. (Bert) Minett was born on the shores of the Muskokas in 1880. When he was an adult, he went to Michigan to work for John Hacker and returned to Canada in 1910 to set up his own business, the H. C. Minett Boat Works. One of the early boats he built was a 31-footer on commission from a Pittsburgh family who spent the summer in Muskoka. The craft was long and narrow and proved to be the fastest boat on the Muskoka Lakes. An order for another boat soon followed from a Buffalo resident who also vacationed in Muskoka. Minett created a slightly faster 32-footer with a cedar hull (this was before ubiquitous mahogany planking) and a Van Blerck engine. She was operated by a two-man crew.

Around 1917 Minett provided electric starters and navigation lights on his boats. Minett, like his mentor John Hacker, was an artist with little business sense. It was said he sold boats for $6,000 that had cost $7,000 to build. He also overexpanded his shop, and bankruptcy loomed. In 1925 he was saved by 25-year-old Bryson Shields, a socialite who knew all the well-to-do summer colonists. Shields bought into the company and became the business and sales manager of Minett-Shields.

Minett's launches stayed mainly in the Muskokas and other nearby lakes, partly because they were produced in small numbers, about 15 each year. He had the highest reputation of all the builders of the area. He wanted always to build the best and would use the best materials and construction. Sometimes Minett fiddled interminably with

The *Areta II*, a 1930 Ditchburn 23-footer. *Classic Boating*

seemingly insignificant details or reworked things that seemed already perfect. During the boom years of the 1920s, some of the affluent families who spent their summers around the Muskokas would pay Minett-Shields prices, which were a third higher than Ditchburn's prices.

Although Minett-Shields also built V-bottom boats to order, it concentrated on large displacement boats—the knife-on-edge variety that cut through the water—up to the 1930s. Minett built a 30-foot displacement boat for James Royce, a relative of the Royce of Rolls-Royce, in the early 1930s. The boat had a Rolls-Royce engine, and the Rolls-Royce radiator-cap "spirit of ecstasy" was mounted on a light fixture near the bow. It was long and thin with a double cockpit aft of the engine.

Minett also introduced a round-bottom boat that had its bottom flattened toward the stern so it could move more quickly than the straight displacement boats. In other words, it was a semi-displacement boat.

The ultimate Minett boat was probably the Hacker-designed, 39-foot, triple cockpit, two-step hydroplane runabout *Wimur II*. Minett-Shields built it in 1929, and the

A 1932 34-foot Minett boat is typical of the builder's conservatism. *Classic Boating*

The 22-1/2-foot *Top Hat*, one of the last Ditchburn boats, was built late in 1937 just before the company's demise.
Classic Boating

boat received wide coverage in boating magazines. Apparently Hacker's home company did not object to this outside work. Perhaps he gave it a percentage of the fees, or maybe because these builders were outside the United States, they were outside the scope of his agreement with the McCreadys.

Port Carling

The first Muskoka boats produced en masse were the powered skiffs of the Disappearing Propeller Boat Company. The Dispro boats were also used on Georgian Bay, although they weren't as popular in its more exposed waters. They were successful in the numerous rivers and lakes of the Canadian North, and were shipped to the United States, England, Ireland, China, France, and Brazil. The company advertised itself as the largest boatbuilder

in Canada. All this success led to the establishment of a U.S. company in 1920 with its plant in North Tonawanda, New York, and its offices in Buffalo. The Muskoka boats were not hugely successful in the United States, and the American company went out of business in 1923. The Dispro company in Canada followed suit in 1925, doomed by the outboard motor. A good example of a Dispro boat is on display at the Muskoka Lakes Museum in Port Carling.

Several men who had been interested in the Dispro company formed the Port Carling Boat Works in 1927 to produce small stock boats with a simple form of assembly line. Initially the boats, called SeaBirds, were a slightly larger version of Dispros: powered skiffs with square sterns and without the disappearing propeller. As time passed the boats became more and more like runabouts. Port Carling occasionally built custom runabouts.

A 1936 SeaBird by the Port Carling Boat Company. Although this company first produced simple powered skiffs, it built triple cockpit runabouts by the mid-1930s. *Classic Boating*

Greavette

Tom Greavette, a director and one of the founders of Ditchburn, left the company and set up his own plant in 1930. This was a double blow to Ditchburn. It lost a strong executive and gained a strong competitor in a decidedly limited market. Greavette must have felt that his involvement with the *Rainbow* racing boats Ditchburn had developed for Harry Greening was strong enough that he was entitled to call his company Rainbow Craft. Using that name, it advertised that it would mass-produce stock boats. Ditchburn, nettled by Greavette's use of the name, objected so strongly that the new company became Greavette Boats Ltd.

The Great Depression in Muskoka

Ditchburn collapsed in 1932, in the midst of the Great Depression. It struggled back in 1933 and opened a smaller plant. Other builders coped as best they could. The Greavette company set up assembly lines and built launches on a mass production basis. It produced the boats very well, but few people wanted to buy one. Greavette floundered, then reorganized in 1933. After the reorganization, it announced a new commitment to John L. Hacker

and a return to custom boat building. This arrangement lasted through 1937.

Port Carling Boat Works didn't cut wages or lay off employees during the Depression. It was the only large Muskoka boatbuilder and one of the few anywhere not to do so. The company continued to produce stock models of lighter and less expensive boats than those from Greavette's unsuccessful assembly line. Port Carling was financially sound enough that it established another plant at Honey Harbour on Georgian Bay in 1935.

In 1936 Ditchburn failed again and was reorganized.

The market for Minett-Shields luxury-priced boats evaporated for a time in the early 1930s, but the builders were back in business by 1933. The company made smaller boats in the 18- to 26-foot range that were mainly designed by Hacker. By this time, Minett had lost all ownership in the firm, though he continued to be the production chief until World War II.

Greavette and Ditchburn each built boats for the new 225-cubic-inch racing class and shipped them to Toronto. In 1935 Greavette built a custom runabout with a torpedo stern, the 33-foot *Curlew*, that was designed by John L. Hacker. Hacker made several trips to supervise the boat's

During the Depression, many companies unsuccessfully tried to sell small, glossy boats. *Covana*, a 1932 Dodge 16-foot runabout, was built by the failing Horace E. Dodge Boat & Plane Corporation. It was an attractive model that sold at a low price, but the boat still could not save the company. *Classic Boating*

construction. Once he brought an expert builder from the United States to demonstrate to Greavette's employees how the streamlined curves should be put together.

By the mid-1930s, the Port Carling Boat Works built more launches than most of the Muskoka custom builders combined—up to 50 a year. Ditchburn failed for the third time in 1938 and did not rise again. Port Carling, by then said to be the largest boatbuilder in the British Empire, bought Ditchburn's unfinished hulls and completed the boats in its own plant.

Muskoka, like the Thousand Islands of the upper St. Lawrence, nurtured boatbuilders. In addition to the larger companies, builders including Barnes, Borneman, Brown, Duke, Matheson, and others turned out a small number of excellent boats. Most had nothing like the overhead of the major boat shops, and many were able to scrape through the Depression.

Economic Recovery
Chris-Craft

At the end of 1935, Chris-Craft showed a profit for the year. The company raised wages five percent in 1936, but

in 1937 it began to pay for its fame, its location in the Detroit area, its association with the auto industry, and its financial recovery. The United AutoWorkers picketed the plant and shut it down. The Smith family, out of necessity, signed a contract with the union, but after that felt alienated from their workers and the town of Algonac. Strikes that occasionally followed did nothing to heal the breach.

Chris-Craft's construction methods allowed it to enter into the 1938 market with 105 boat models, almost all equipped with Chris-Craft engines. Its engines were produced in such numbers and were so popular that they were sold separately to other boatbuilders and owners. In 1939 the company increased its output to 115 models and established a large branch plant in Holland, Michigan. The production line in Holland began at the end of November.

Despite the emphasis on mass production, the Smiths occasionally built semi-custom boats. In 1936, at the request of a group of European sportsmen, Chris-Craft produced fast 18-foot runabouts that became a one-design racing class on the Riviera. In the following years, 16- and 19-foot "Special Race Boats" were offered for customers who wanted to race runabouts elsewhere. From the depths of the Depression until World War II, Chris-Craft also produced a small number of 26-foot Special Race Boats. They looked much like normal 26-foot runabouts but were lighter and more heavily powered. Their engines were 850 cubic inches, the maximum size allowed in runabout races, but were tuned to produce 100 horsepower more than the normal engine of that size. The boats were not listed in a catalog. They were only available to people whom the Smiths or their dealers were satisfied could safely handle the boat. Wolves in runabouts' clothing, they could outstrip most entries in speedboat races.

Chris-Craft produced its most streamlined runabouts in 1941. One model, the barrel-back, was similar to others built by Gar Wood and Century. It had a flat transom in a half-rounded shape, and the sides of the boat had an extreme tumblehome aft. The relatively narrow afterdeck had considerable crown to meet the rounded transom, suggesting the unfortunate name that implied clumsiness rather than streamlined grace.

On October 2, 1941, the labor union, which had signed a two-year contract with Chris-Craft 10 months prior, went on strike and had unusually tough pickets that let no one, including the company officers, into the plant. Water lines, sprinkler systems, and boats left in the open could all be damaged in the cold weather. It took more than a month before a court issued a restraining order prohibiting "threats of violence or intimidation" and effectively ended the strike.

Chris-Craft had some government contracts, and shortly after the Japanese attack on Pearl Harbor, it received so many more contracts that there was no room to build pleasure boats.

Hackercraft

The Hacker Company started to emerge from the Depression in 1935. One of its first moves was to offer a utility boat once again—a tribute of sorts to Lyman, although unlike Lyman's, the boat was smooth-skinned and made of varnished mahogany. The company also offered several sizes and designs of attractive runabouts, all designed by John Hacker, who was their captive designer of stock runabouts. His stock boats were moderately streamlined, but he never produced the extreme barrel-backs and barrel-bows. However, some of his custom boats and racers were built as streamlined torpedoes. In 1935 the Hacker company received a loan of $20,000 from the Reconstruction Finance

Athena, a 1933 Gar Wood 28-footer, was one of four such boats sold that year. *Athena* still has its original six-cylinder 200-horsepower Scripps engine that provides a top speed of 40 miles per hour. *Classic Boating*

nearby pier. The driver revved up the boat in a series of figure eights and drove against the pilings at top speed, again and again, striking with one side and then with the other. The next day Huber visited the Lyman plant and was lucky enough to meet Bill Lyman. He described what had happened the day before with the idiot and the boat. Bill Lyman laughed, "*I* was that idiot." Periodically he took a boat off the line and tested it that way. Then the boat was taken apart in the shop, piece by piece, to see what might have happened to it—a stringent method of quality control.

World War II affected every aspect of life, and Lyman contributed to the war effort. By 1942 Lyman used all its facilities to build boats for the war.

Century

The Century Boat Company located in Manistee, Michigan, rose gradually in 1932 from obscurity and bankruptcy to become an important builder for the pleasure boat market. Century, a builder of outboards, after its recovery and new ownership, began to build inboards. There were two Sea Maid runabouts, a 15-foot, 11-inch model and a 17-foot model, that had top speeds of 27 and 31 miles per hour, respectively. Century also offered a 14-foot, cockpit-aft Thunderbolt hydroplane runabout capable of 45 miles per hour. By 1933 there was an additional Sea Maid—a company name for family boats that became well known. All Sea Maids and Thunderbolts had varnished mahogany hulls. The advertising slogan was "Going Strong with New Models and Lower Prices"; some of the boats sold for less than the comparable Chris-Crafts.

Frank Newman, Century's purchasing manager at that time, remembered that lumber and new engines often sat on railroad cars on a Manistee siding until enough boats were sold to make enough money to meet the sight-draft bills of lading. The suppliers weren't ready to extend credit to the company.

Unlike the other major builders who used double planking on the bottoms of their stock boats, Century used their own, less expensive "Air Cushion Hydraulic Bottom." It had overlapping bottom planking—essentially lapstrake, running

Corporation—a government organization that bolstered faltering businesses after the Depression. As the Depression eased, the company sold enough boats to carry it through to World War II when it built boats for defense.

Gar Wood

The Wood factory built 295 boats in 1937, the year of the first Chris-Craft strike when Chris-Crafts were not available. This amount was the most the company would produce until World War II. Gar Wood continued to introduce new models, including streamlined designs with new barrel-bows, in extremely small numbers. The barrel-bow runabouts look dated today, perhaps more so than boats built earlier, but they were not as ugly as the name suggests. The term echoed the earlier unfortunate "barrel-back" description and the bows did not look anything like barrels. The hull was a little fuller at the bow than in previous models, and the general effect could be more heavy than graceful, but it conformed to the streamlined fashion.

Lyman

In 1933 Lyman offered 17-, 19-, and 23-foot, white-painted lapstrake boats. The company flourished, and in 1937 the Lyman operation moved to a larger plant in Sandusky that had a modified production line. That year they produced between 500 and 600 boats. Some were sold as tenders for large steam yachts. Lyman boats were shipped to Europe, South Africa, and Indo-China, but most went to the U.S. recreational market.

Bob Huber was a crew member on a power cruiser that had come into Sandusky. One day in his early teens, he stood in the Battery Park Marina and watched some crazy drunk smash a Lyman against a group of pilings off a

The Depression led to smaller and simpler boats, and the start of a major change from runabouts with cockpits and engines under hatches to utilities—open boats with engines inside under boxes. *Buddy*, a 1937 Chris-Craft 17-foot Deluxe Utility, powered by a Hercules 55-horsepower Model B engine, exemplifies the change. *Classic Boating*

fore and aft—fastened by copper rivets. The overlap provided strength and was said to help level riding.

By 1941 Century advertised 47 different models, including the new boats—"barrel bow and stern"—that most builders offered as streamlining became fashionable. The catalog also included several utilities. Most of this fleet was powered by Gray or Universal engines, while a few had Ford V-8s. That year was Century's grand prewar climax. They soon moved to wartime construction and built tens of thousands of assault boats.

The End of a Golden Age

The adult life of Christopher Columbus Smith largely coincided with what are often called the Golden Years of powerboating—an age that ended with the beginning of World War II. Luke Stephensen, a Chris-Craft employee,

Empress, a 22-foot Gar Wood Streamliner, was built in 1939. Streamlining became popular in the late 1930s. The "barrel-back" form—a half-circular transom and afterdeck curved to fit—was adopted by several stock builders. Notice that the difference of the internal layout between runabout and utility was fading. *Classic Boating*

A Gar Wood 22-foot Streamliner of 1941, *Tahoe Tessie*, shows the barrel-bow. *Classic Boating*

Sweet Louise, a 1942 Century 20-foot triple-cockpit Sea Maid, was one of the few such boats by Century and was probably the last one before World War II. *Classic Boating*

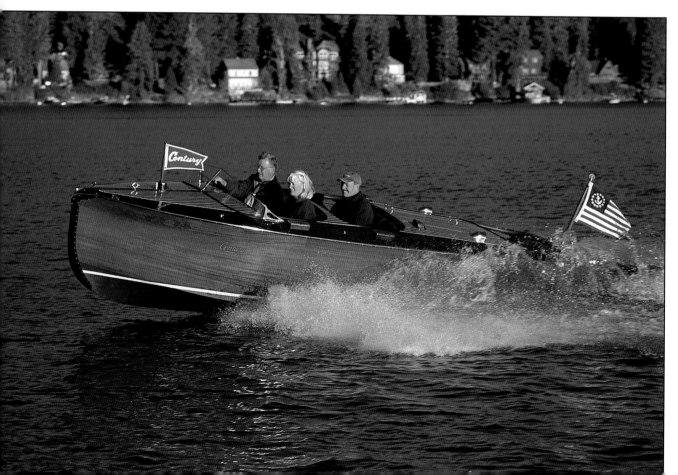

The 1941 Chris-Craft runabouts of 17, 19, and 23 feet were fashionably streamlined. They were still relatively small Depression-era craft. *Chris-Craft Collection, Mariners' Museum, Newport News, Virginia*

told Smith's final story in an interview with Jeffrey Rodengen. One day in 1939, Stephenson came to work and found Chris Smith sitting on a nail keg outside the Chris-Craft plant's boiler room, one of Smith's favorite resting spots in his later years. Blood smeared his shirt from a nosebleed that wouldn't stop. Stephenson called Jay and Bernard Smith. They put their father in a car and started to leave. They put the car in reverse, backed up all the way to the boiler room, and blew the horn. Stephenson came out and

Chris said, "Luke, keep a damn good head of steam. Where I'm going I don't want to freeze." Everyone laughed and his sons drove him to the hospital. He had massive ulcers of the nasal passages, perhaps from his years of smoking cigars. Two weeks later, despite a series of blood transfusions from members of the Smith family, he died. He was 78 years old. The man who personified development of the powerboat more than anyone else was gone.

CHAPTER 4

CRUISERS AND COMMUTERS

The 55-foot commuter *Thunderbird*. The outer planking is made from Honduras mahogany, and the inner diagonal planking is cedar. Note the art deco trim at the bow and along the side. The cabin is stainless steel. Designed by Hacker and built at Bay City, Michigan, she was launched in 1940 and shipped to Lake Tahoe. A later owner added the bridge shelter and converted the boat to a high-speed cocktail lounge. *Classic Boating*

Cruisers and Commuters

Sailing yachtsmen had cruised on the Great Lakes for years. In the early 1900s, it was adventurous to cruise them in motorboats. In 1901 one such cruise was on the *Betty*. The boat was a 40-footer built in De Pere, Wisconsin, and was launched on the Fox River. She had a two-cylinder, four-cycle engine, a fantail stern, relatively high sides for rough weather, and a long cabin over most of her length with a partially raised wheelhouse near the bow.

The cruise started at Green Bay. The three-man crew consisted of a professional captain, an engineer, and the owner, James Strawbridge, who acted as cook. They left by night, "pushing into a stiff breeze with whitecaps breaking all around us," recalled Strawbridge, and cruised to Little Sturgeon Bay. The next day they went to Gladstone, Michigan. There, the following morning, they took on iron pigs because the launch was greatly in need of ballast.

The local manager of the Cleveland Cliffs blast furnaces suggested that he accompany them on his boat, the *Nepenthe*, as far as the lightship. Strawbridge was invited to have lunch on *Nepenthe* during that part of the trip, and he went aboard her after he warned the *Betty*'s engineer not to run too fast because the new engine was not yet broken in. The engineer couldn't stand being left behind as *Nepenthe* moved out smartly at her maximum 11 miles per hour, and the two boats continued side by side until the engine on *Betty* developed hot journals and stopped.

Nepenthe turned around and took *Betty* in tow for the 17-mile trip back to Gladstone. Soon *Nepenthe*'s people began to bail water from her engine room because she had burst a water discharge pipe. *Betty*'s engine had by this time cooled down and was able to run slowly, so both boats limped back to port under their own power. Luckily the blast furnace had a good machine shop where the *Betty* spent the next two days because "the brasses had to be refitted, the wrist pin scraped, and general overhauling" of *Betty*'s engine, said Strawbridge.

During *Betty*'s next jump, the sun went down, the wind came up, and Strawbridge said they got "such a rolling and pounding as made us truly glad to see the harbor lights of Manistique." The next day they headed for Mackinac Island, but rough water came up that was so unpleasant that they headed into Naubinway for shelter. Three days later, after a stop at Mackinac Island where Strawbridge sent a telegram to his wife who was waiting for him at St. Joseph Island, they reached Detour. A man there hailed *Betty* as she came in and asked if Strawbridge was aboard. Mrs. Strawbridge had not received her husband's telegrams and had become so worried about his failure to appear that she asked this man, a Mr. Hare, to send out a tug to look for him. After Strawbridge talked to Hare, the *Betty* moved briskly up the St. Mary's River to the Raines Hotel, where Strawbridge's wife and friends waited.

Hull Evolution

The development of the internal combustion engine changed the shape of boats. Early cruisers such as the *Betty* were displacement craft. In an effort to use evolving engines that could drive the boats faster than before, and to keep the usual fantail sterns from squatting at speed, designers produced various types of hull shapes. A hull that was broad and flat aft to resist settling

A 1939 Hacker cruiser owned by Montague Black, a Canadian. *Classic Boating*

In the early 1900s, small power cruisers were simple. This 1909 example is in the Georgian Bay island area. *J. W. Bald Collection, Huronia Museum 967-166-024*

in the water, with finer lines toward the bow, eventually became the standard. If driven fast enough, a boat with this hull would plane. Unlike the designers of racing boats and runabouts, cruiser designers had to produce a heavier vessel and balance speed against seaworthiness, passenger comfort, and operating cost. To move a cruiser at planing speeds, powerful engines that used a great deal of expensive fuel were required. These engines and their fuel tanks took up a lot of space at the price of passenger accommodations, so most cruisers had limited speed compared to lighter craft.

As the bottoms of hulls gradually changed, so did the topsides. Raised decks forward were developed around 1905. They provided more enclosed space, were easier to build, and were stronger because the deck beams could go across the entire boat without a break for the cabins. The boats also handled easily in the seas.

The Matthews Boat Company

The Matthews history is a capsule history of wooden power cruisers. In 1890 Scott J. Matthews started his boat-building career in the basement of his home in

Bascom, Ohio, near Toledo. He may have been the first to inspire the standard joke about amateur boatbuilders: When his boat was completed, it was too big to go through any door or window. Eventually part of the building's foundation was cut away and the boat was moved out of the basement. He decided to improve on that model, built another in a shed in his father's lumberyard, and looked for a buyer.

Matthews placed a small advertisement in the *Toledo Blade* that a Toledo resident named Burwell answered. Burwell was an engineer for the Cleveland Bicycle Company, whose headquarters was in Toledo. Burwell purchased the boat and decided to install one of the new gasoline engines. He used a do-it-yourself kit and built the engine in the bicycle machine shop. Matthews was profoundly unsatisfied, and as a result, he installed some naphtha engines in his boats.

H. A. Lozier was a Toledo entrepreneur who made a fortune as owner of the Cleveland Bicycle Company. He had recently sold it and was interested in engines for cars and boats. Lozier asked Burwell to explore the compact steam and gas engines being produced, and he asked Matthews

36-Foot Open Water Cruiser
Design No. 3602

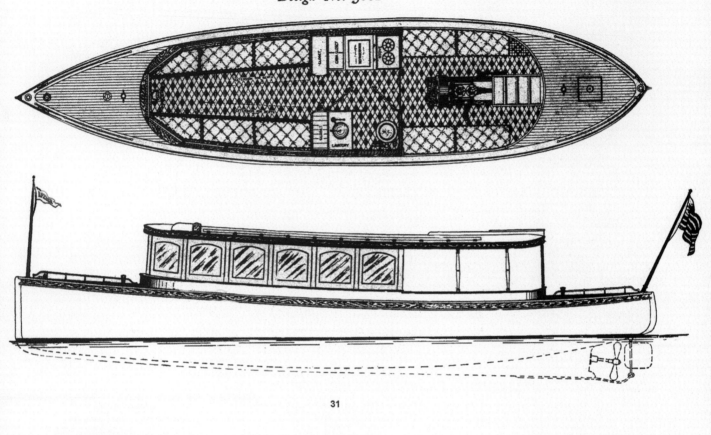

31

An early Lozier 36-footer of the type built for Lozier by Matthews. *Antique Boat Museum*

for a boat demonstration. Lozier was a heavy person, and the boat was a long, thin toothpick. Lozier wanted a boat more suited to his proportions and ordered a wider boat. In 1898 he established the Lozier Motor Company in Toledo; he intended to build small marine motors himself and sell boats made by Matthews. As the Lozier company grew, Matthews developed a sizable boat-building shop in Bascom. According to a 1900 Lozier catalog, the boats ranged up to 50 feet in length. Lozier put some naphtha engines into the craft, but he soon produced and installed his own internal combustion engines.

To modern eyes, the Lozier engines seem tiny in proportion to the boats they powered. In the 1900 catalog, Lozier offered single-cylinder, two-cycle engines from

1-1/2 horsepower to 8 horsepower. The catalog said, "One turn of the fly-wheel starts the electric sparking device, and one small spark explodes the vapor within the cylinder." A description of the boats' construction from the catalog reads:

Our boats are made to form the best combination of reliability and speed. We use only the best material, white oak for frame, and cypress or cedar for planking; copper fastened and clinched; all nail holes plugged with red cypress. All joints and seams are fitted with the accuracy of cabinetwork, and so designed as to combine light, yet thorough construction.

The Matthews cruiser *Vamaheka* was built in 1908. Matthews boats at that time had displacement hulls and often were canoe-sterned. The tall stack is in the background. *Warren S. Weiant III*

In 1900 the Lozier company moved to Plattsburg, New York, on Lake Champlain. Lozier apparently felt that Lake Champlain, with its connection to the Hudson River and its proximity to New York City, gave the company better access to the Atlantic Coast and European markets. Burwell had worked at Plattsburg as a superintendent at a sewing machine factory and liked the city.

In the December 1900 issue of *The Rudder*, there is an account of a 31-1/2-foot Lozier boat that traveled 900 miles from Toledo to Plattsburg. An illustration shows its graceful hull with a sedan-like enclosure that ran the length of the boat, except for a small deck at the bow and

a small cockpit at the stern. A 6-horsepower, two-cycle, one-cylinder engine drove her. On board were "Mr. Burwell and companions."

Burwell and crew ran into heavy weather on Lake Erie, "the waves at times breaking over the boat from stem to stern," the article reported, but "at no time was there the slightest trouble with the engine; an average speed of 7-1/2 to 8 miles per hour was easily maintained." The first day, they went from Toledo to Lorain, with a stop at Put-in-Bay. The next day they went on to Buffalo where they entered the Erie Canal on their way to Lake Champlain.

Matthews built the *Detroit* in 1912 especially for a transatlantic voyage. Driven by a two-cylinder Scripps engine, she made the crossing in three weeks. *Dossin Great Lakes Museum, Detroit*

had a large open passenger area forward, with the usual flat canopy held above it on slim poles, and a cabin aft. It was the exact reverse layout of most cruisers. Although she had a galley, a head, and two sofa-berths, she was primarily a day cruiser, which explained the unusual layout. Men and women in Edwardian dress could sit on wicker chairs in the open front area and see the Muskoka scenery.

Matthews began to specialize in cruisers. He turned out a 60-footer for Edward Ford of Toledo in 1907. She had a tiny raised deck forward that was attached to a short forward cabin, which contained two sofa-berths and allowed access to the engines. The engines were immediately abaft the cabin, under a deck over the usual top, held on poles. The control station was at the forward end of this deck. The helmsman had a horizontal steering wheel, about the size of one on a truck, that stood at the end of its vertical shaft. A long, low trunk cabin was behind that deck. Lengthy padded davenports that could be converted to berths were along each side of the cabin. The head and galley also were under the cabin.

A Matthews to Cross the Atlantic

One of the more remarkable Matthews products, a 35-footer designed to cross the Atlantic, was built in 1912. It was commissioned by W. E. Scripps, the many-talented commodore of the Detroit Yacht Club, publisher of the *Detroit News,* and owner and engine designer of the Scripps Marine Motor Company. The boat's purpose was to display the virtues of the Scripps motor and the reliability that marine engines had finally achieved. As a newsman, Scripps knew the boat should be small enough so its crossing would attract worldwide attention.

The boat was named *Detroit* and was a heavily built double-ender that resembled a lifeboat. It had two bunks tucked into a small forward cabin that had six feet of headroom. The engine room in the aft end was about the same size as the forward crew's quarters and also contained a berth for the engineer. The boat was powered by one of Commodore Scripps' engines; a two-cylinder model built in Detroit that moved her at 5 to 6 knots. Amidships there was

Matthews Alone

Matthews continued to build Lozier boats for a while and shipped them to Plattsburg, where Lozier engines were installed, but H. A. Lozier Sr. also hired a Plattsburg boat-builder named Frederick Milo Miller. Miller had spent his apprenticeship with a Scottish builder in Glasgow. Henry Lozier Sr. died in 1903, which may have ended Matthews' dwindling connection with the Lozier company. The Matthews Boat Company in Bascom, Ohio, began to advertise on its own in December 1903 in the Detroit-based boating magazine *Sail and Sweep.* Matthews was now in competition with Lozier, who had advertised there for the preceding year.

Lozier's sons were interested in cars, not boats. In 1905 the first Lozier car was exhibited in New York, and the Loziers' connection with boats ended. Miller set up his own boat shop on Lake Champlain. Matthews was now alone on Lake Erie.

Matthews' health was poor, and on doctor's orders he took a long vacation. His 74-foot double-ender *Onward* carried him and his family 9,000 miles down the Mississippi River, around Florida, up the East Coast, and eventually back to Lake Erie through the Erie Canal.

The Move to Port Clinton

When Matthews returned to Lake Erie, he decided to build only custom boats. In 1906 he moved to Port Clinton and set up a new plant. One of the first boats he built was for F. R. Moodie, of Hamilton, Ontario, to use on the Muskoka Lakes. (The first powerboats on the Muskokas were brought in from outside.) The boat was a narrow 51-footer with a canoe stern and a 30-horsepower engine. She an open deck; the steering wheel was at its forward end. No engine controls were at the steering position—a technical limitation of the day. The person in charge of maneuvering the boat had to call out commands through an open hatch to the engineer standing in the engine room. This procedure caused few problems in open water, but it was clumsy when maneuvering in tight places.

Five stainless steel fuel tanks were tightly fastened in under the deck amidships and held 1,000 gallons of gasoline. Two additional hundred-gallon tanks and some small containers were mounted on deck, so she carried a total of 1,275 gallons when she started out. It was announced in advance that no smoking was allowed on board because of all the gasoline. An additional tank of unspecified size held extra lubricating oil and was stored in the engine room. *Detroit* carried 200 gallons of water and stores for 90 days. She had a tall mast rigged so that she could use her sails, which were produced by a Chicago sailmaker, to steady her or, in case of a breakdown, to sail her into port.

With her crew of four, including her captain, Thomas Fleming Day, an experienced small craft sailor and editor of *The Rudder,* the *Detroit* started her journey from Detroit on July 12, 1912. She passed through Lake Erie, the Erie Canal, the Hudson River, and Long Island Sound and arrived at New Rochelle, New York. From there, she headed across the Atlantic on July 16. Every two or three days, the engineer stopped the engine to check it over. Otherwise, except for one occasion when some water got into the fuel, it ran steadily. *Detroit* arrived with an exhausted crew at Queenstown (present-day Cobh), Ireland, on August 7. After a break to rest and reorganize the crew, she went on through a peaceful Europe to St. Petersburg, Russia, and made port there on September 13.

The Largest Matthews Boats

In 1913 Matthews built the first diesel-powered yacht on the Great Lakes. It was a 110-footer with the tongue-twisting name of *Aeldcytha.* The next year Matthews launched the commuter *Marold,* a 100-footer for C. H. Wills of Detroit, the chief engineer of the Ford Motor Company. The boat had four

V-12 Van Blerck engines that drove her up to 30 knots. It was a round-bottom, semi-displacement boat, as were most boats by Matthews. She had a raised forward deck over half her length that extended into a trunk cabin that ran most of the remaining length and left only a small open cockpit at the stern. A windshield and an overhead awning protected her bridge, which was amidships on top of the raised forward deck. The bridge could be enclosed at the sides by canvas curtains. The exhaust from the engines was vented into a stack just abaft the bridge. Although Matthews built this large commuter and a few other speedy boats, he wasn't very interested in express cruisers and did not produce many ultrafast craft.

The company expanded during World War I and changed its name to the Matthews Company. It built 110-foot submarine chasers and airplane hulls, presumably for flying boats. The hulls were shipped without wings to the East Coast.

Matthews Stock Cruisers

In 1924 Matthews introduced its first stock boat, a 38-footer. All five boats were sold to Ford Motor Company officials before they were completed. The Matthews plant finished its last custom boat, the 99-foot *Irwin,* in 1925.

The company introduced a 46-foot stock cruiser in 1926 and a 32-foot speed cruiser in 1928. In 1930 Matthews produced slightly more than four stock cruisers each week and worked year around. The company employed about 250 people; a separate department made dinghies for the cruisers. Among the models that Matthews announced for 1932, the single-cabin 38's house structure was given "trimmer lines." It wasn't exactly streamlining, but it was a slight move in that direction.

The 100-foot *Marold* of 1914, powered by four Van Blerck engines, was built by Matthews for a Detroit owner. *Mystic Seaport, Rosenfeld Collection, Mystic, Connecticut*

In 1925 Matthews began to make stock boats exclusively. *Ranger* was a stock 1930 Matthews 38-foot, single-cabin cruiser. *Classic Boating*

Rumrunners

In 1920 Prohibition was imposed on the United States. People along the Detroit, Niagara, and upper St. Lawrence Rivers and other rivers that separated the United States from Canada took every model of boat from skiffs to commercial fishing boats to the Canadian side. There they filled them with booze and lugged it back to the United States. The Michigan towns of Ecorse, Lincoln Park, and Wyandotte and Alexandria Bay on the St. Lawrence River became smuggling centers.

Well-organized racketeers soon muscled out individual entrepreneurs in the smuggling business located along the Detroit River. Bodies of the less-experienced lawbreakers would turn up floating in the river. The Purple Gang from Detroit became involved.

As rumrunners became more professional, they wanted faster boats to outrun the authorities. Although only a few of the smuggling boats are known today, legend says that most of them were runabouts. No doubt some

were, but runabouts could not carry much cargo and didn't handle well in rough water. One smuggler who relied on pure speed unwisely tried to cross Lake Ontario in a hydroplane and disappeared forever beneath the waves. Although a scattering of rumrunners were disguised as commercial fishing boats, most of the illegal craft seem to have been high-powered cruisers large enough to carry cargo. Al Capone owned a Robinson cruiser-commuter, but whether he used it for business or pleasure is uncertain.

The Prohibition law was generally disliked, and boatbuilders probably felt slight concern about who used their craft. Smugglers throughout the centuries have had a romantic appeal, and their association with fast boats only added to the boat's attraction—the faster the boats, the greater the attraction.

The Burger Boat Company

In 1915 the Burger Boat Company in Manitowoc, Wisconsin, was incorporated. Its history went back to

1892, and the family occupation as boat- and shipbuilders went back to 1857. The company had built cruisers since 1901, when it turned out the 85-foot, clipper-bowed steam yacht *Vernon Jr.* for Vernon Seeber of Chicago. Steam and gasoline yachts up to 150 feet and tugs and fishing boats soon followed. During World War I, Burger built vessels up to 110 feet long for the war effort.

After World War I, in addition to custom orders, the company made stock boats and concentrated on a standard 36-footer in 1920 and 1921. The boat had a raised deck forward, a trunk cabin aft, and a central bridge deck with an overhead awning and side curtains. According to *Motor Boat* magazine:

> The specifications show a form of construction and selection of materials which compare very favorably with individually built cruisers of high class. It is in equipment that the standardized boat compares to advantage with boats built separately. This is because the entire matter of design, construction, equipment, and furnishing is done by the builder, and each item of equipment is selected as a result of thorough understanding of the service expected.

Burger advertised the boat as "A 50-foot Ship—36 feet long." A photo feature in the magazine showed that the boat had comfortable accommodations and suggested the advertisement wasn't far fetched. One simple reason for the ample accommodations was that this was a family boat and didn't have the crew's quarters that would have taken up space in the 50-footers of the day. By the early 1930s Burger offered cruisers ranging from 28 to 46 feet.

Chris-Craft

Chris-Craft gingerly entered the express cruiser market in 1929 and produced four 48-foot stock boats described as commuters; each was powered by two V-8 engines.

Boating enthusiasts had become fascinated with luxurious, superexpress yachts and the life they provided their owners. One account in the February 1929 issue of *Motor Boating* told how the owner of a large commuter left his Long Island home each morning and walked down to the

dock to his craft, accompanied by a young man who was his secretary. As soon as he boarded, the great cruiser was underway. The owner took a shower, shaved, and dressed in fresh clothing laid out by the valet-steward. Breakfast was served and his morning newspaper was laid beside his plate. He ate, read the paper, and dictated some letters until the boat drew up to a downtown New York landing. When they disembarked, he and his secretary went directly to a waiting car that took them to the office.

Chris-Craft had grown successful by making people's dreams come true at affordable prices, and introduced its 38-foot Commuting Cruiser in 1929. It was a stock boat with a forward cockpit behind a curving windshield, a trunk cabin, an open bridge, and a short afterdeck. The boat could travel at 30 miles per hour and was priced at $15,000. She had sleeping accommodations for four, a galley, and a head. Her engine was a newly produced Chris-Craft 250-horsepower V-8. The topsides were varnished mahogany and continued the Chris-Craft style. The boat was a beauty and a great success; the company sold 65 of them through 1931, and some still exist. It is doubtful that the majority were actually used to commute, but the boats were fast and maneuverable, and the owners could imagine themselves as commuting tycoons. The term "commuter" soon became synonymous with "express cruiser."

The Defoe Boat and Motor Works

In 1905 at Bay City on Lake Huron, high-school principal Harry J. Defoe, who was fascinated by boats and the water, quit his job and established the Defoe Boat and Motor Works. Defoe's business partners were his brother Frederick, a lawyer, and G. H. Whitehouse, who was in the wholesale fish business. Whitehouse knew boats and their uses and probably steered business to the new boatyard.

Harry Defoe began his business when he converted sailing fish boats of the region to the gasoline motors that the fishermen wanted. Defoe then built small, powered fish boats. Bay City already had two companies that provided "knockdown" boats to amateur builders. Defoe also built

Big Chief, one of Chris-Craft's 38-foot commuting cruisers, was introduced in 1929. These so-called commuters—express cruisers often not actually used for commuting—were fashionable status symbols, and 65 were sold. *Classic Boating*

knockdown kits that contained all the necessary parts to build a boat. The pieces were precut, test assembled, taken apart again, and sent to the eager amateur to re-assemble and fasten together. At some point, this aspect of the business was split off and became Bay City Boats, Inc. It grew into the largest operation of its kind in the country, and shipped knocked-down boats to every state and several foreign countries, including the government of the Philippines. As boat design developed over time, the de-signs of the kit boats evolved, and John Hacker prepared some of them.

During the early years, Defoe built an 18-foot launch that had a 3-horsepower engine that sold widely. By 1912 he turned out custom-built cruisers up to 65 feet long. He built a 65-foot cruiser in 1915. A report of that time said, "The construction is of the usual heavy and stanch Defoe type, the frame being entirely of white oak, and planking of Louisiana red cypress." She had a canoe stern, and a cruising speed of 12 miles per hour and was intended as a "deep sea cruiser" for its Toronto owner. World War I gave Defoe his first large boost, with government con-tracts for five wooden 40-foot "spent torpedo chasers." A later contract for eight steel 98-foot steam mine planters led the company to the hurried erection of a steel shipyard.

Bay City had long been a center for shipbuilding, and the necessary skilled workers were not hard to find.

The advent of Prohibition brought government con-tracts to companies equipped to build rumrunner chasers. In 1924 and 1925 Defoe built 15 wooden 75-footers and 12 steel 100-footers for the Coast Guard. This placed him in the business of building fast yachts, vessels often over 100 feet in length.

Gar Wood

There was a small group of owners to whom expense meant little and speed a lot, and they wanted attractive boats that would be impractical for most uses. Gar Wood was as interested in fast cruisers as fast boats of every other kind. In 1920 he produced *Gar Jr. II*, a 50-foot express yacht powered by two Gar Wood Liberties. He shipped her to Florida where she won all the cruiser races. Wood decided to race the Atlantic Coast Line train, the *Havana Special*, along the coast from Miami to New York. He beat the train by 21 minutes. After that, Wood set a new speed record on the Hudson River and continued on to Detroit. The speed king must have been frustrated while he worked his way through the locks of the Barge Canal en route to Lake Erie. The editor of *Motor Boating* was along for the ride with Wood.

Defoe, whose products ranged up to large yachts, built at least four of these 55-footers in the mid-1920s from a Hacker design. *Historical Collections of the Great Lakes, Bowling Green State University*

The Disadvantages of an Express Cruiser

After Wood arrived home, he left Algonac shortly afterward and headed off on the boat with a social party on a cruise to Lake Superior. Traveling through Lake Huron, they met almost every kind of nasty weather, but after they loaded fuel, supplies, and charts at Sault Ste. Marie, they went on to Lake Superior where the weather was better. Wood was interested in exploring Superior's northern shore; he poked into uninhabited pine-shadowed coves and discovered small hamlets. He fished and bought fish from commercial fishermen they occasionally met.

The great disadvantage of an express cruiser that traveled along an isolated, semi-wild coast was soon evident. By the time the boat came to the town of Jackfish, a bit past the middle of the northern shore, her fuel tanks were almost empty. The town was the only place for many miles that had a rail connection, and Wood hoped gasoline was available there.

The railway stationmaster had one 54-gallon barrel of gas that a more foresighted yachtsman who expected to come that way during the summer had shipped in advance. The 54 gallons would take *Gar Jr. II* another 40 miles closer to civilization to Rossport, which might have a better supply of fuel. Wood coveted the barrel of fuel, but the stationmaster refused to let him have it. As an inducement, Wood offered him a voyage to Rossport, and he accepted only if he could get a replacement for the barrel's contents. The stationmaster used his telegrapher's key and eventually arranged amounts that varied from 5 to 15 gallons to be shipped in from stores along the railway. When he was sure that these would replace the amount in the barrel, he accepted the trip for himself, his family, the local storekeeper (his brother), and his family. Unfortunately, no eastbound trains were scheduled that day to stop either at Rossport (to pick up the returning party) or at Jackfish (to take them back home).

In those days, the railways tried to be helpful, and after an explanation by way of the telegraph to Canadian Pacific headquarters, a transcontinental train was ordered to carry the Jackfish residents home from Rossport. *Gar Jr. II* took only an hour to reach Rossport, and no doubt gave the guests a memorable experience. At Rossport Wood bought enough gas to get the boat to a more developed port.

Gar Jr. II was the first of possibly 10 boats of the same pattern—referred to as Gar Jr. Flyers—that Wood built between 1923 and 1928. The well-heeled purchasers, who used them as cruisers or commuters in fully inhabited areas, had no worries about scarcity of fuel. One boat was sold to Marshall Field of Chicago, and another went to H. N. Torrey of Detroit.

Gar Wood produced about 10 Gar Jr. Flyers in the 1920s, and used one himself. Two V-12 Liberty engines powered most of them. *Mystic Seaport, Rosenfeld Collection, Mystic, Connecticut*

Wood's Ultimate Commuter

In 1923 Wood built a 70-foot commuter for L. Gordon Hamersley of New York. He fitted her with five Gar Wood Liberty V-12 engines, which provided a top speed of 50 miles per hour. *Motor Boating* commented, "That such a combination of size and speed were possible would have been denied by most boatbuilders a few months ago." The fifth engine drove the center one of three propellers and could be used alone to maneuver the boat in harbor. Two flank propellers were driven by two engines, which were equipped with clutches so they could be used together or alone. Long and lean, with only a small deck structure and a raised deck forward, this boat was a seagoing greyhound that some consider a forerunner of the fast PT boats of World War II. Hamersley, a tobacco magnate, named her *Cigarette*, which remains a name for fast boats today.

The engines could not be controlled directly from the bridge. An engineer stationed in the engine room operated them. A full-time engineer was probably needed anyway to maintain the bank of engines. According to *Motor Boating*,

In *Cigarette,* the captain's orders are carried to the engine room from the bridge through three marine telegraphs of the usual type, as in all large yachts, passenger vessels and commercial boats. The engineer need not leave his position facing the telegraphs to operate the controls, reverse gear levers, etc.

Cigarette was a 70-foot commuter built by Wood for tobacco millionaire L. Gordon Hamersley in 1923. The boat was driven by five V-12 Liberty engines. *Mystic Seaport, Rosenfeld Collection, Mystic, Connecticut*

When *Cigarette* delivered her owner to his Wall Street offices and rushed toward her East River landing at full speed, the striking performance was such an attraction that traffic on East River Drive would stop. Hamersley sold the boat back to Wood two years later, supposedly because his wife was scared of it, and bought one of the less powerful 50-foot Gar Jr. Flyers. Wood renamed the 70-footer *Gar Sr.*, removed some of the engines, and added additional deck cabins, and it served as his own yacht for many years.

Great Lakes Boat Building Corporation

The Great Lakes Boat Building Corporation was organized in Milwaukee in 1915. Although it produced runabouts and small pleasure fishing craft, it concentrated on building cruising boats. In 1916 it offered a 48-foot express cruiser, with one-man control and comfortable and luxurious accommodations for a party of eight and a crew of two. If 10 people ever actually cruised in comfort on a 48-footer, even though the two-man crew was restricted to tiny living quarters, they must have known each other very well. With advertising hyperbole aside, the boats were well built and comfortable for a reasonable number of people. The 48-footer was truly fitted out in luxury. An advertisement said, "A novelty in the main cabin aft is a built-in Victrola concealed in a cabinet in a most attractive and ingenious manner." Most Great Lakes Boat Building cruisers were in the 40- to 50-foot range and traveled at about 20 miles per hour. Henry Ringling, the circus impresario, bought a 48-footer that could move at 22 miles per hour. These boats had standard designs that could be built to order and included any changes the customer wanted.

The Great Lakes Corporation also created many custom designs. In 1916 it produced *Kingfisher*, a 56-foot express cruiser for E. L. King, who demanded that his new boat had comfort, convenience, and speed. The boat's speed was not published, but it was provided by two newly designed Van Blerk engines. The interior was certainly comfortable for all but the crew, whose pipe berths were hung in the engine room, where they also had their own head—a common arrangement in those days.

Developments at the Great Lakes Boat Building Corporation contrasted with the developments at Matthews. Great Lakes provided a few standard cruisers, although apparently not many were constructed in advance as stock, as well as custom boats. In 1923 Great Lakes offered a 45-footer and a 54-footer but was willing to stretch the 54-footer to 65 feet if an owner wanted that length. One who did was Philip K. Wrigley of Chicago, whose boat was named *Wasp II* (in those days the name had no sociological or ethnic meaning). The *Wasp II* had an eight-cylinder Sterling that produced a speed of 27 miles per hour. Her layout followed a pattern that became standard for larger cruisers, with raised deck forward, a combined wheelhouse and lounge amidships, and a trunk cabin aft.

Great Lakes Express Cruisers

The Great Lakes Boat Building Corporation built a variety of boats to order. *Miss Liberty II* was a 62-footer made for a Buffalo resident. Two Sterlings moved her at 30 miles per hour. Her controls were all at the wheel. "It is indeed an indication of a high state of development when one man can handle a 62-footer with a powerplant developing 600 hp," reported a 1920 *Motor Boat* magazine.

In 1920 Great Lakes launched *Frances*, a 104-footer billed as the "Largest Express Power Cruiser," for John F. Dodge, the automotive giant. *Frances* just edged out Matthews' 100-foot *Marold* from 1914. As a result of test-tank experiments while she was being designed, *Frances* reached 30-plus miles per hour and was pushed by four 400-horsepower Murray & Tregurtha engines that drove three propellers through special gearing. The boat was built of wood but had a steel hogging girder that ran from stem to transom—a metal backbone to keep the boat from drooping at the ends. She had double planking with mahogany outer planking. The inside paneling also was made out of mahogany; her inner decks were covered with Wilton carpeting and her upholstery was imported broadcloth.

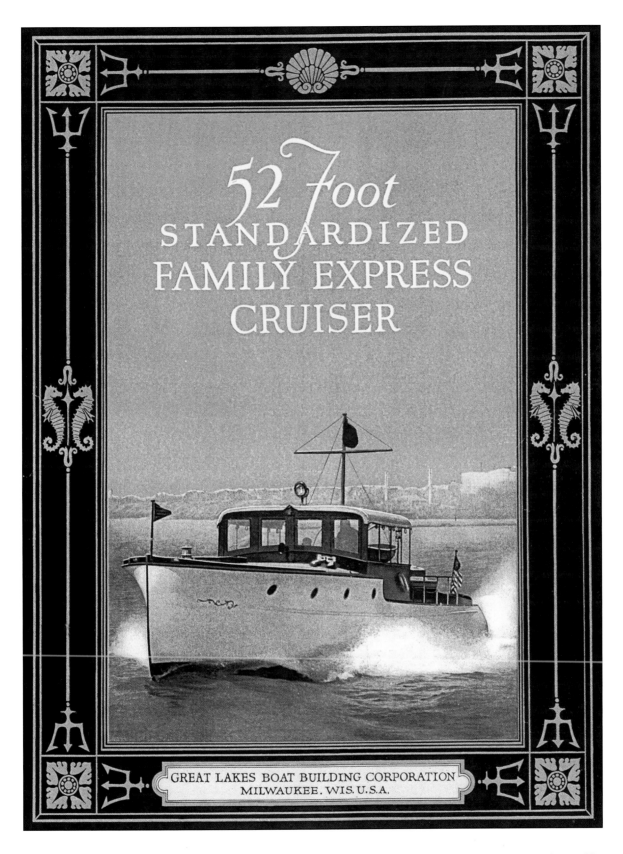

52 Foot
STANDARDIZED
FAMILY EXPRESS
CRUISER

GREAT LAKES BOAT BUILDING CORPORATION
MILWAUKEE. WIS. U.S.A.

The front cover of a Great Lakes Boat Building Corporation catalog from around 1915. *Milwaukee Public Library/Wisconsin Marine Historical Society*

Frances had a long raised deck forward, a dining and lounging saloon raised partly above the deck amidships, a raised and enclosed bridge, an engine room, two double staterooms with heads and showers, and quarters for a crew and a captain. John Dodge died before the boat was completed, but the Dodge estate took the delivery and decided she met all requirements. Her price was not divulged, but she was quickly sold and was soon renamed *Adroit II*.

Great Lakes also built *Pam*, a slightly more modest but equally unusual boat. She was a 62-foot "Combination Cruiser and Day Boat" built for a member of the Hiram Walker Distillery family in Detroit. Harrington F. Walker wanted to use her for day trips and for commuting between his home in Grosse Pointe and his Detroit office. He also wanted to cruise to Georgian Bay on fishing jaunts. *Pam* followed a pattern unusual for boats of her size but similar to that of many smaller cruisers. She had living quarters under a trunk cabin forward and a helmsman's position just aft of amidships on the long open afterdeck with the usual top held on supports. She carried her 14-foot power tender on deck forward on the starboard side, in a large notch let in to the forward cabin. The galley was located in the cabin just off the afterdeck, which had room to seat a sizable afternoon party. The afterdeck also could be closed in by canvas side curtains when the weather was bad. Her speed demonstrated what now could be achieved by large cruisers. Driven by two six-cylinder Sterling Petrel engines, she could travel at just over 22 miles per hour.

John L. Hacker

John L. Hacker designed cruisers during most of his long career. In 1922 he joined William Fermann of New York City to form a company that acted as yacht brokers and designed large custom cruisers, which were built in yards other than Hacker's. Hacker was the designer and Fermann was the business operator. Their custom boats were among the first to have twin controls—one set on the bridge, the other in a wheelhouse-saloon. The boats probably originated the walk-around deck. Hacker and Fermann also advertised 55-foot cruisers, which were built to a standard plan. Two Kermath 100-horsepower engines through twin screws drove the boats, and their maximum speed was 15 miles per hour. Several were built, most of them by Defoe. The boats had two staterooms and a head aft under a trunk cabin and an enclosed wheelhouse-saloon. The galley, crew's quarters, and head were forward under a raised deck. The crew's quarters were sufficiently comfortable that they could be used as an additional stateroom. This was in contrast with many designs that skimped on crew comfort. Although Hacker continued to design cruisers, the

Flying Cloud, a 39-foot Robinson Seagull cruiser-commuter from 1928. It was designed by Hacker and luxuriously outfitted. *Flying Cloud* was owned by Ransom E. Olds of Oldsmobile fame and was named for his biggest and best car. *Classic Boating*

partnership with Fermann was dissolved in 1926. It probably had become evident that Hacker contributed to the enterprise more than Fermann, and Hacker, who was prosperous at the time, bought him out.

Hacker's Express Cruisers and Commuters

Hacker designed and built the "40-foot Super-Speed Cruiser" *Mary K.* for a Detroit owner in 1920. On an enlarged V-bottom runabout hull, the boat had cabins over what would be forward and aft cockpits on a runabout. The controls were in the forward cabin, which had two seats, and one could be extended to a double berth. Aft of that was a railed open deck, and under that were two six-cylinder Hall-Scott engines that drove the boat 30 miles per hour. Farther aft was the main cabin. Its entrance was a sliding hatch and companionway from the open deck. The cabin contained two sofa beds, a provision for an upper berth if necessary, a compact galley, and a head.

Hacker progressed to a different form of fast cruiser. He designed the commuter *Comet,* which was built in California in 1922. He designed *Via Water,* a 50-footer driven by two V-12 Liberty converted aircraft engines in 1923. In 1926 Defoe launched the 85-foot, Hacker-designed commuter *Rosewill.* Two V-12 Packards powered her, and the bridge had every possible item of contemporary navigational equipment.

In 1930 Hacker launched a 38-foot cruiser-commuter for the King of Siam. The boat had solid gold fittings in the cabin and was paid for with gold bullion. The boat was driven from an open front cockpit and powered by a 12-cylinder Packard engine of 650 horsepower, working through Hacker reduction gear. Its speed was timed at 63.73 miles per hour, the fastest boat of its type afloat.

The Hacker Boat Company introduced a stock 38-foot commuter-cruiser in 1930. It was not a gold-fitted boat, but otherwise it was very similar to the king's, including the control station in an open front cockpit. Two Kermath engines of 225 horsepower each powered the boat, which gave a speed of 42 miles per hour. About a year later, he introduced a similar 35-footer, powered by two Gray 140-horsepower engines. Hacker continued to design large custom boats until he died, but few were as flamboyant as his commuters.

The Purdy Boat Company

In 1922 the Purdy Boat Company, at that time located in Trenton, Michigan, produced *Shadow F.* It was a 72-footer the company described as an "Ultra-Express Cruiser" with two 12-cylinder Allison engines that drove the boat at 35 miles per hour. The forward cockpit could seat six people on hand-buffed Spanish leather upholstery. Within the cabins, there were equally luxurious accommodations for six people. The boat had been built for Carl G. Fisher, who owned the Indianapolis Speedway, was an officer in the Allison Engineering Company of Indianapolis, and made a great deal of money in the development of Miami Beach. His office was in New York City.

Fisher found the Purdy brothers working in an East Coast boat-design office and set them up so they could build racing boats for him on the grounds of the Indianapolis Speedway. He moved them to a plant in Miami Beach in 1917. In 1921 he moved them to Trenton, Michigan, where *Shadow F* was built. In 1925 he moved the Purdys to Long Island. The description of *Shadow F* in the October 1922 issue of *Motor Boating* ran across four heavily illustrated pages that emphasized her luxury and power. At the end of the description, the article stated that Mr. Fisher had ordered another boat and was selling this one. The last paragraph asked that inquiries be sent to Fisher at his New York office. The makeup and typeface of the piece were similar to a regular magazine article, but if the reader looked carefully, the word "Advertisement" was in tiny letters at the bottom of each page.

The Richardson Boat Company

The Richardson Boat Company in the Buffalo suburb of North Tonawanda built 29-foot raised-deck boats by 1910, and within the next few years, it produced a 26-foot, raised-deck, V-bottom cruiser that could travel at 14 miles per hour. A standing roof or awning held in place by supporting poles was often fitted over the open deck aft. This arrangement became the pattern for many cruisers of many builders in the following years. During World War I, Richardson built small cruisers of this type, as well as several 64-foot motor tugs, for government use.

Richardson built a custom V-bottom 45-foot express cruiser in 1920 that was designed by William H. Hand, a well-known advocate of the V-bottom. A six-cylinder Sterling engine, built in Buffalo, powered the boat. Other boats of various types followed.

Richardson Stock Boats

Boating magazines promoted the idea that builders should produce stock boats. In 1919 and 1920 *Motor Boat* magazine emphasized that idea and had William Deed, a naval architect, design a 26-foot cruiser adapted to stock construction. The cruiser was christened the *Scout*, and the next issue of the magazine said Richardson would build the *Scout* and a 23-foot version as standardized boats in 1921. Both were chunky and round-bottomed and followed the pattern of a raised deck forward, aft of which was an open deck covered by a canopy. The smaller and more popular boat had a speed of 9 miles per hour, and they both were powered by a compact four-cylinder engine, the Gray Z marine motor.

In 1926 Richardson produced 50 of its 23-footers. Many were shipped to Florida, which was an up-and-coming resort area. A new sales manager had joined the company, and whether he brought new ideas or was hired because Richardson had the new ideas is uncertain. In the fall of 1926, the Richardson company advertised a 34-foot cruiser and two 23-foot cruisers at sale prices "to make room for the 1927 standardization schedule." This schedule centered on a 26-foot Richardson Cruisabout, designed by Eldredge-McInnes, a naval architecture firm in Boston. The most obvious change in this design was the move away from the raised forward deck that replaced it with a cabin trunk. Designers had begun to realize the raised deck forward made small boats look ungainly. The control station, just abaft the cabin trunk, had a windshield and small side windows attached to the top.

In 1928 Richardson introduced a 28-foot Master Cruisabout. She had the same Gray engine as the smaller

boat and had a guaranteed speed of 11 miles per hour. She sold for $3,585—a considerable jump from the price of the discontinued 23-footer. In 1929 the 28-foot hull was offered with five possible accommodation plans, ranging from a day cruiser to a double cabin boat. Stock production was well established. Builders of cruisers remained conservative in their general styling, and Richardson boats continued to have vertical windshields.

The Rochester Boat Works

In 1916 Volney E. Lacy established the Rochester Boat Works on Lake Ontario at the mouth of the Genesee River, according to its historian William Lindquist. Lacy was said to have been trained at "Massachusetts Tech" as a naval architect and marine engineer. In the late 1910s, Lacy, who remained president of Rochester Boat, brought in Bernard C. Meiers as manager. It is hard to say which man's vision produced the attractive boats that followed.

Rochester Boat Works mainly built standard cruisers, although it offered a few runabouts. By 1919 Rochester advertised several models, including a 45-foot standardized express cruiser with an enclosed bridge and a raised deck forward. This was a layout Rochester followed for all but its smallest cruisers. The enclosed bridge was a novelty and of course drew the complaint that it diminished visibility from the boat's control station, but it quickly became popular.

In December 1921, *Motor Boating* published a photo spread of a Rochester 50-footer, and said of the combined

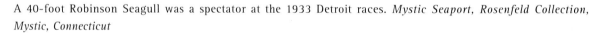

A 40-foot Robinson Seagull was a spectator at the 1933 Detroit races. *Mystic Seaport, Rosenfeld Collection, Mystic, Connecticut*

In 1930 Hacker built this 38-foot commuter for the King of Siam. Its cabin fittings were solid gold. Powered by a Packard engine of 650 horsepower, it traveled at over 63 miles per hour. Hacker produced stock commuters much like this, but without the gold fittings and with less powerful engines. *Author's collection*

pilot house, lounging saloon, and dining room, "It can be made as comfortable as an open bridge, and in case of inclement weather, can be transformed into a water-tight cabin in a few moments." Rochester later advertised that it was the "Originators [sic] of the Standardized Enclosed Bridge Cruiser," and no one protested. Before long, many builders of cruisers used the feature on everything except the smallest boats. This 50-footer was driven by two Van Blerck four-cylinder engines, and like Rochester's other boats, it had a concave V-bottom.

In the early 1920s, a Rochester catalog listed three runabouts and nine cruisers; the latter ranged from 33 to 75 feet long. There were no photos of the 62-, 65-, and 75-footers, so they may never have been built. A. W. MacKerer, the boatbuilder and naval architect who left Chris-Craft after a disagreement in 1923, joined Rochester that year and remained there until he went back to Chris-Craft in 1926.

The Robinson Marine Construction Company

Glen Robinson established the Robinson Marine Construction Company at Benton Harbor on Lake Michigan in 1925. In the midst of the 1920s boom, he saw a market for fast, luxurious boats among an upmarket clientele. The boats were sleek and powerful and had varnished mahogany hulls. Their brand name was Seagull. Beginning in 1927, Robinson offered a speedy 36-foot model. In 1929 it added a similar 39-foot boat.

John Hacker designed these cruiser-commuters for Robinson. They were something like the cruiser-commuters that his own company soon offered. However, the control station of each Robinson boat was at the front of the enclosed sedan cabin, rather than in the open forward cockpit of the Hackercraft. The terms we use today to describe boats of the past were not necessarily used as carefully then. An advertisement for "The Beautiful Robinson Seagull" in the November 1928 issue of *Yachting* referred to the Hacker-designed 39-footers as "these fleet, graceful runabouts."

The 39-foot cruiser was described in the May 1929 issue of *Motor Boating*. Behind the helmsman's station in the cabin, there were a head, galley, and four Pullman berths that could be pulled down at night. Like most such craft, this one had an open stern cockpit with wicker chairs and a roomy, well-cushioned seat. The boat was equipped with one or two Hall-Scott or Sterling engines. The maximum advertised speed was 32 miles per hour. Also advertised was

A 1928 Richardson 29-foot cruiser. *Antique Boat Museum*

a 39-foot Red Arrow day-cruiser version of the boat that was driven by twin screws. This was the commuter model, described by Philip Moore as "a fast, elegant, reliable boat sold to commuting yachtsmen not only on the Great Lakes, but on the East Coast as well." Some of these commuters may have had open control stations in forward cockpits such as those in the later Hacker commuters.

Robinson's cruising 39-foot Sport Sedan was first shown in January 1930. The hull was unchanged, but the controls were moved from the forward cabin to an open bridge aft of the cabin. The cabin was shortened and the space that had been the helmsman's position was turned into a sporty forward cockpit. The aft cockpit remained for pleasant-weather seating.

That same year, Robinson offered a 40-foot Speed Cruiser and a 45-foot Custom-Commuter. Like the revised 39-footer, these boats had controls on an open bridge that were protected only by a windshield and useful aft cockpits. The Speed Cruiser was probably designed by Walter Leveau, the company's in-house architect. The boat was advertised to have speeds up to 35 miles per hour. It and the 39-footer remained on the company's list for several years and alternated in its advertising. Although the models were almost the same length, each apparently had its own appeal to customers. By the next January, Robinson also advertised an "entirely new" 36-footer. It was the earlier Hacker design

but now had an open bridge. Two 250-horsepower Hall-Scotts powered the 45-footer. It was also available as a double-cabin cruiser—the second cabin was placed where the aft cockpit was located on the commuter.

Robinson Expansion

Robinson Marine expanded constantly during its early years. In 1929 it announced that it had built 25 large craft the previous year and planned to build 50 that year. By 1930 it had a plant where 24 boats, many of them sizable, could all be constructed at the same time. It advertised under a stylized sketch of a seagull with the words "Often seen but seldom passed." The phrase "At Yachting's Smartest Rendezvous" was added in a 1930 advertisement. In 1930 Robinson wisely began to branch out and produced 22 Coast Guard rum chasers that were 36-1/2 feet long and guaranteed to go 32 miles per hour.

Robinson still looked toward the well-to-do for customers. He did not advertise that one very rich customer was Al Capone. An advertisement in the May 1931 issue of *Yachting* was more fitted to appear in the glossy pages of a society magazine. "Swift and true as the arrow whips from the bow, your Robinson Speed Cruiser or Commuter will cover the miles with the precision of perfectly synchronized marine power tuned to match the cushioned ease and rugged strength of an oak-ribbed hull."

The Great Depression

During the Great Depression, people who still had some money may have thought it was wiser to invest in tangible things, such as boats, than in stocks or banks, either of which might collapse. Even so, the Depression struck builders of runabouts hard. People who had money were reluctant to flaunt it by buying speedy mahogany launches. Commuters were even more out of fashion. Fast, varnished, and conspicuous boats were no longer wanted when workers sold apples on street corners or stood in line at soup kitchens. However, white-painted cruisers were different, even though they might be able to reach considerable speed. Sales of varnished mahogany express boats almost disappeared, but most builders of plain cruisers profited because their boats didn't look as flashy.

Matthews

Matthews prospered, and its best years were 1930, 1934, 1936, and 1937. During this time, it turned out an average of 100 cruisers per year. By 1941 Matthews produced four lengths of stock cruisers; the largest was 50 feet long. After 1941 Matthews produced landing craft and patrol boats for the war effort.

Richardson

Richardson inspired an article in the March 15, 1931, issue of the *New York Times* that said the company's plant worked 10 hours a day, six days a week. A completed cruiser went out the door every day.

In 1932 Richardson offered a 26-foot Utility Boat that was completely open except for small decks at bow and stern. The hull was of a size and type that allowed the purchaser, at any future time, to add cabins and convert it to a cruiser. In 1935 it produced the Scouter, a 20-foot open boat. It was advertised as "A big, husky workboat for fishing, ferry and yacht tending."

In 1931 Richardson inaugurated the Sailaway, a yearly event that continued until World War II. People who had purchased Richardson cruisers from the East Coast arrived one day in early May and took over their new boats—as many as two dozen of them—and in a convoy skillfully managed by the company, they proceeded from the Niagara River via the New York Barge Canal and the Hudson River to New York City. Mother-hen Richardson briefed the owners (most were entirely new to boating) the evening before, had an executive in the boat that led the convoy, had a small gasoline tanker follow the lead boat, oversaw the boats' passage through the locks, planned the stops at night, took care of refueling and refilling water tanks, and finally turned the flotilla loose at the mouth of the Hudson. The Sailaways generated a great deal of publicity and perhaps cost the company less than it would have spent if it had shipped the new boats directly to their owners' home ports.

The Richardson company produced its first double-cabin boat in 1931. The main cabin was aft of the bridge and there was a smaller forward cabin. In 1932 the first Richardson boats with sloping windshields appeared. One 1935 model, the 28-foot Streamline Richardson Jr., had a

The *North Star II* was a double-cabin Matthews from 1930. *Mystic Seaport, Rosenfeld Collection, Mystic, Connecticut*

completely streamlined cabin. The forward ends of trunk cabins were sloped, and corners were rounded slightly on all the 1936 models. The company had announced that its boats were modishly "speedlined." By 1937 Richardson had become the world's largest producer of medium-sized standardized power cruisers.

In February 1937 G. Reid Richardson died. He was president, treasurer, and general manager of the company. A series of reorganizations happened after his death.

In 1941 two new models were introduced. The largest was a 36-footer that had a total of four hulls with various arrangements available within each one. By July of that year, Richardson sales reached new heights, but the plant soon had to be converted to build a variety of war craft.

Burger

The Burger Boat Company produced the first steel cruiser, the *Tamarask*, in 1938. Up to that time, the company had considerable experience in making wooden cruisers and welded steel fish tugs. In 1941 it built the 65-foot, flush-deck, steel cruiser *Pilgrim*. These boats were forerunners of the large welded-metal pleasure boats that Burger built after World War II.

Chris-Craft

The Depression almost swamped Chris-Craft in 1932 when runabouts, its basic product, stopped selling.

Three 1937 Chris-Craft models of 26, 29, and 40 feet. Chris-Craft's runabout and commuter business almost ended during the Depression, but the company saw that cruisers sold well. *Chris-Craft Collection, Mariners' Museum, Newport News, Virginia*

Commuters became unfashionable at the same time. Buyers had liked commuters because they made them feel like important people even if they didn't commute by boat to their offices. Even the people who still could afford to buy expensive and fast boats found that conspicuous speed no longer seemed desirable.

The company changed its cruisers from varnished commuters to simple, white-painted, 31- and 36-foot models. These boats had trunk cabins forward and raised canopies over large cockpits aft. They looked like everyone else's cruisers.

By 1934 Chris-Craft adapted to the change and offered a 24-foot sedan—advertised as "a moderately priced cruiser that had everything"—for $1,495. In the Depression, this was real money. The boat had a Chris-Craft rubber-mounted motor.

As the Depression eased, Chris-Craft expanded its cruiser fleet. By 1937 it offered boats that ranged up to 40 feet with a variety of cabin arrangements. In 1939 the company expanded the Holland, Michigan, plant that was its main cruiser source. By 1940 the company produced 11 lengths of cruisers that ranged up to 55 feet long. Chris-Craft, the largest and most powerful boatbuilder, had weathered the Depression and now competed head-on with established cruiser builders.

Gar Wood

Gar Wood offered a 26-foot cabin cruiser in 1935. The company built 26 of them that year, but the numbers fell off quickly in the following years. His larger fast cruisers no longer had a market. His company survived because of his own millions. Soon after the Depression, the company began defense work for the war effort.

Great Lakes

The decline of Great Lakes started before the Depression. Essentially, the company concentrated on building custom boats and did not emphasize its standard models. The company didn't change with the changing market as others did, and it was in poor financial health. In 1923 several Chicago yachtsmen, including Philip K. Wrigley, announced that they would invest a million dollars in the Great Lakes Boat Building Corporation, with the intention of moving it from Milwaukee to Chicago, where it would go into volume production. W. C. Morehead remained the president.

The company appeared in a Chicago listing in 1924, but it actually operated in Milwaukee until 1926. That year, the Milwaukee boatyard was listed as occupied by Henry C. Grebe, boatbuilder; residence: Chicago. In the 1928–29 listing in Chicago, the Great Lakes Boat Building Corp. showed

Henry C. Grebe as president and M. L. Grebe as secretary. In a separate listing at a different address, Henry C. Grebe & Co. (a firm already widely known as yacht designers) added "boatbuilders" to its description and had the same two men in the same two positions. Over the next few years, Great Lakes mainly produced stock boats that Grebe designed. Eventually the Great Lakes boatyard disappeared and a Grebe boatyard appeared. A financial listing shows that Great Lakes' stock was worthless by 1941, but the Grebe yard continued to build large pleasure boats for some time after World War II.

Hacker

During the 1930s John Hacker lost control of his own boat company but continued to design runabouts and utilities for it. The company continued to use his name as part of the title, but it seldom credited him with the designs he produced. During that decade he designed the racers and runabouts for which he was famous and also is said to have designed 70 cruisers, most built outside the Hacker Company's plant. One of them was the 65-foot *Barat,* which was powered by the first pair of GM diesel engines.

Hacker designed the *Thunderbird*, a commuter/cruiser and the ultimate art deco boat. The Huskins Boatbuilding Company of Bay City, Michigan, built her. Launched in 1940, she was shipped by rail to her owner, George Whittell, of Lake Tahoe. Her 55-foot mahogany hull with an inner, diagonal layer of cedar was built over alternating sawn and steam-bent oak frames. The *Thunderbird* was essentially a giant speedboat that had the convex bottom Hacker had first used on his runabouts. Her deckhouse was a streamlined carapace of stainless steel welded and riveted together. The control station was at the front of this structure like the pilots' compartment in a passenger airplane. Secondary controls were at the midships boarding entrance. Powered by twin Kermath V-12 Sea Raider engines, she had a top speed variously stated as 43 or 45 miles per hour. Some reports also give her a pair of smaller secondary engines for harbor maneuvers, but that is uncertain. A later owner added a windshield, partial enclosure, and full control station at the midships location to make it the bridge. The owner also removed the after cabin and cockpit to provide a large open deck aft, and converted the interior from sleeping quarters to a high-speed cocktail lounge. Now powered by two V-12 Allison engines, the *Thunderbird* remains on Lake Tahoe today.

Hacker continued to design cruisers, but his private fortunes were bleak. In 1940 he lost his comfortable suburban home, and thereafter he and his family lived in a succession of smaller houses in Detroit.

Lyman

There was an unusual entry into the cruiser market in the 1930s. Lyman, in Sandusky, Ohio, had produced outboard boats, but during the Depression the market for them disappeared. Casting about to keep afloat, manager Bill Lyman began to build small, white, open, clinker-built inboard launches that he called "utilities." They proved to be quite successful.

Thunderbird was originally built in 1940. The 55-foot, Hacker-designed commuter was piloted from the front of the stainless steel cabin much like an airliner. With Hacker's convex V-bottom and two 12-cylinder 500-horsepower Kermaths, its top speed was 43 to 45 miles per hour. A later owner added a bridge structure and removed the aft cabin and cockpit, which left an open afterdeck. *Hacker Collection, Mariners' Museum, Newport News, Virginia*

At that point, he took on almost any job to keep going. Apparently enough people wanted cruisers that he produced four custom boats, all carvel built. The *Seagull*, a displacement 40-footer built in 1935 and originally equipped with a 120-horsepower Sterling Petrel engine, provided a top speed of 10 miles per hour and still exists at the Antique Boat Museum in Clayton, New York. *Mary Jeanne II,* a 48-footer, had a semi-displacement hull and could travel at 22 miles per hour. Lyman built two others, which kept his workmen occupied but probably didn't make much profit.

Robinson

Plans for an unusual boat appeared in *Power Boating* in June 1932. The magazine said, "Show visitors will remember the very beautiful mahogany craft which was exhibited by the Robinson Marine Construction Company at Grand Central Palace last January. For want of a better name it was called a 'sport boat.'" It was 32 feet long and had an open front cockpit with two rows of seats and a small enclosed cabin amidships containing a tiny galley and a head; aft of the enclosure the cabin sides and roof were extended to shelter part of the aft cockpit, where seats ran along each side. It looked a lot like a miniature commuter.

Robinson's hometown newspaper, the Benton Harbor *News-Palladium,* had announced the boat the preceding January. "The new sport model has been developed during the last six months according to designs by W. A. MacKerer, and previews have disclosed a craft that for sheer grace and snappy contour has no equal." That statement followed an announcement in the December 1931 *Motor Boating* that MacKerer had joined Robinson as vice president and general manager in charge of construction and design. MacKerer had been a driving force at Chris-Craft but had been laid off during the Depression. He later returned to Chris-Craft in 1935.

The boat was advertised with "a variety of arrangements." One arrangement had a true sedan cabin amidships and smaller open cockpits fore and aft, which made it look even more like a small commuter. It was a Depression-era attempt to build a less expensive craft that still had Robinson character. Unfortunately, its size placed it in the runabout class and its appearance made it a commuter—the two types of boats that no one wanted to buy. The number of these 32-foot craft that were produced is unknown. An August 1933 Robinson advertisement offered "Four Distinguished Commuter Models." They were a 39-foot sedan cruiser (the Hacker design), a 39-foot sport sedan (the Hacker boat with an open raised bridge), a 40-foot sport cruiser, and a 45-foot custom commuter. All these models had been carried forward from earlier years.

A local news story from September 1935 reported that 27 boats were being built at the Robinson plant and that the company had just received orders for 13 Coast Guard 26-foot cutters. In 1936 a notice in *Motor Boating* announced that Robinson was going to specialize in custom-built craft. This probably meant that glossy, fast stock boats no longer sold well and that the company would only build pleasure boats to order.

Robinson, however, had become the Tiffany of boatbuilders. The company retained its connections with the few people who were very rich, knew what they wanted, and cared little about fashion. In July 1936 *Power Boating* published a list of the seven pleasure boats that Robinson was building at the time. They ranged from a 23-foot sport

fisherman to a 54-foot cruiser. Some of the owners lived in Chicago, and some were in Texas.

Orders for deluxe pleasure craft could not sustain the company. In September 1936, a Benton Harbor newspaper reported, "Twenty-seven motorboats of various sizes are now under construction at the Robinson Marine Construction plant." Thirteen of the boats were for the Coast Guard, and 14 were for the Coast and Geodetic Survey.

In 1937 Robinson built at least 10 (the number was vague) boats that were said to be for a French company or for the French government. The company ambiguously announced: "The boats are intended for pleasure and business purposes, and are being used at various French resorts and other watering places." Glen Robinson's comment in November 1937, after a trip to Europe, that "he expected to get another contract for more of the fast cruisers which his plant turned out last summer for the French government."

A 33-foot Richardson from 1940. During the Depression, Richardson became the largest builder of medium-sized stock cruisers in the world. *Antique Boat Museum*

Nothing more was published about these mysterious boats and their purpose.

Robinson published an advertisement in 1941 that said although the company was now completely devoted to the defense building program, it looked forward to a return to yacht building for the "Peacetime Fleet of Tomorrow." Robinson wouldn't have any boats in the postwar Peacetime Fleet. The company did not survive long after the end of the war because there was little call for its elegant creations.

Rochester

In 1928 Volney E. Lacy again took full control of Rochester. He took over the main Rochester boat plant while Bernard C. Meiers moved to the uptown store that sold small boats and accessories. Lacy's move back to direct control suggested there were serious problems in the company's affairs—problems that may have preceded the onset of the Depression. In May 1928 the annual *Motor Boating* list of standardized cruisers available showed 10 offered by Rochester, but in 1929 there was none. The only boat advertised by Rochester in 1929 was a 21-foot outboard cruiser, and soon there were no advertisements. Rochester, perhaps already weakened for other reasons, became an early casualty of the Great Depression.

WS 5688 DN

Countdown to Fiberglass

World War II was the beginning of the end for many of the old established powerboat builders. Gar Wood, one of the best known, was the first to go.

Gar Wood

Not many famous businesses closed as rapidly as the Gar Wood boat-building operation after World War II. Anthony Mollica, the Gar Wood historian, researched the story of the company's demise.

The beginning of the end was in 1937 when Wood negotiated an end to the mortgage of his Marysville boat factory with local bankers for a fraction of its amount. He then sold the plant to Gar Wood Industries and combined it with his major company, which made truck bodies and other machinery, and no doubt made a profit for himself.

Wood permitted a plan for the Bus Division to share the factory with what now was titled the Boat Division. This was probably to justify to the company its forced purchase of the boat plant, but it was a move that set the boatbuilders on their ears. The company decided to sell the Bus Division instead, but the boat shop had lost a year's production during the rearrangement. The boat-building operation, Wood's pet for years, now was part of Gar Wood Industries, and he fast lost interest.

Wood owned most of the common stock of Gar Wood Industries, although he depended on his brother Logan, who actually ran the company with great skill. In 1938 Logan died, and Glen Bassett, the former treasurer—who knew how the money the industries made had poured into the owner's boat building and racing—became president. In 1939 Gar sold some of his shares; he sold the remainder

A 1967 Lyman 30-foot Sportsman with its original 318 Chrysler Marine engine. It is equipped with nearly every option then available. Fewer than 50 of these boats were built. *Classic Boating*

Gar Wood boats were produced for only a short time after World War II. *Bonnie Quaich* (Gaelic for "Beautiful Vessel") is a 1946 Gar Wood 18-1/2-foot utility with a Chrysler Crown M-47 engine. *Classic Boating*

in 1941 but became chairman of the board for the duration of the war. After the war, his legendary boat designer, Napoleon Lisee, retired. Perhaps Wood had achieved everything he wanted. He brought in accountants to disentangle his affairs from those of the industries and bought his Detroit mansion back from the company. Then in 1945 he retired.

Bassett remained president when Wood retired. The new board increased executive salaries (Wood had kept them extremely low) and moved to offices in New York. The board hired the noted industrial designer Norman Bel Geddes to design the new offices and then had him redesign all their products, starting with the boats. The boatbuilders, who had prepared striking new designs for postwar production, were not happy when Bel Geddes thought their shop should be overhauled, and were even less happy when advertisements showed their own designs credited to Bel Geddes.

The new regime complained that the boatbuilders wanted to make their boats too good, without competitive pricing. The board said, "It's a shop where boats are made, not produced," and set new, unrealistically high production levels. They also bought the former Dodge factory in

Newport News for the combined production of more boats and gasoline tanks.

The boatbuilders tried hard, and during 14 months in 1946 and 1947, they made nearly 900 boats. Yet in April 1947, management closed the Boat Division. The exact reasons are obscure, but Mollica suggests that resentment of boat building's sacrosanct position and absorption of Gar Wood money over the years had rankled the poorly paid Wood executives so much it was almost foregone that when they could, they would drive a stake through its heart.

Chris-Craft

By contrast, Chris-Craft bought land in Grand Rapids, Michigan, and Jamestown, New York, during the war for a postwar expansion. By July 1946 the company again produced pleasure boats—the 1942 models that could quickly go back into production. Lumber, particularly mahogany, was still scarce after the war, and many of the boats were made of cedar or whatever else could be found. The wood was painted rather than stained, and some angry dealers canceled their orders.

Sentimental Lady, a 1946 Chris-Craft Super Deluxe Enclosed Cruiser, has a model name that seems longer than the boat itself. The 27-footer, produced after World War II when materials still were scarce, brought Chris-Craft back into the cruiser market. *Classic Boating*

The company was busy, and in 1946 it established a runabout plant in Chattanooga, Tennessee. In 1948 it sold the Jamestown plant. By 1953 it produced 111 different boat models. After preliminary work on lapstrake boats in Holland, Michigan, Chris-Craft established a plant in Salisbury, Maryland, in 1954. It was the sincerest form of flattery to Lyman. Similar to Lyman, Chris-Craft produced white-painted lapstrake boats called sea skiffs, the name of traditional lapstrake workboats along the New Jersey coast. In 1955 the company bought the Roamer Corporation of Holland, Michigan, which manufactured steel boats.

The Cobras

That same year Chris-Craft made its first mild venture into plastic construction and produced 18- and 21-foot mahogany boats called Cobras; the upper works were drawn by a designer lured away from General Motors. Each boat had a single high tail fin like an airplane rudder. The tail fins and the plastic hatch covers were made of gold-colored polycarbonate and were matched by gold-colored bottom paint. With deeply curved windshields and bow flagstaffs that leaned backward at a 40-degree angle, the Cobras may

have been inspired by Chevrolet's new plastic-bodied Corvette sports car.

The Cobras replaced an older racing runabout model, and the 21-footers were fitted with Cadillac V-8 engines that could easily drive them over 50 miles per hour. The hull designers should certainly know fast boats, but the Cobras were skittish at speed and sometimes flipped over. The company offered to rework those that were too hard to handle, but only 51 of the smaller Cobras and 55 of the larger were built. By Chris-Craft standards, these boats had poor sales, probably in part because of their poor reputation and in part because the design did not attract buyers. The company was no doubt glad to discontinue the line, but a surprising number of the boats exist today as collectors' items.

Chris-Craft was the world's largest boatbuilder and expanded in many directions, but its company offices remained in Algonac, Michigan, where they had been since the company began. In 1957 the Smith family moved the offices to Pompano Beach, Florida. According to the company, Florida was close to the center of recreational boating, and the weather would permit year-round testing of new models. Today, Florida is either the headquarters or the location

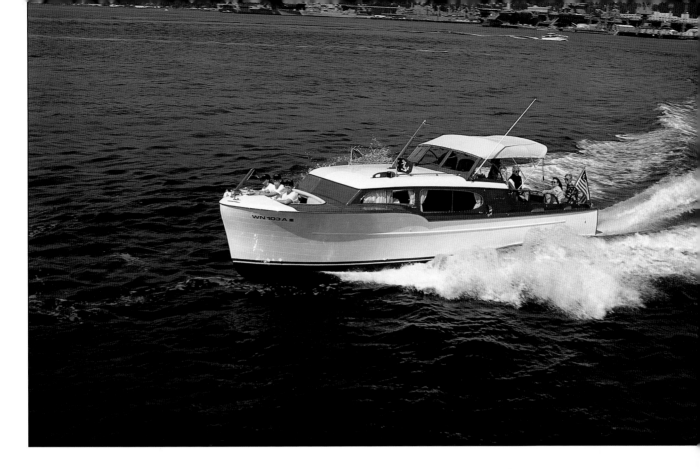

Misty Chris is a 34-foot Chris-Craft Express Cruiser from 1948, when postwar limitations on materials began to ease. *Classic Boating*

of major sales offices for many large boatbuilders, although Michigan has more registered pleasure boats than any other state. Florida taxes were also lower than those in Michigan, and Florida didn't have Detroit's automotive labor unions. The people of Algonac had become more remote, and the Smiths may have been disenchanted with the town they helped develop.

Fiberglass over Wood

In 1957 Chris-Craft bought a company that built outboard boats made with fiberglass over plywood, but the plywood often delaminated and the model was soon dropped. In 1958 the 19-foot inboard Silver Arrow was built and essentially had a planked hull coated with fiberglass on the sides but not the bottom.

In 1958 the company offered 147 models; the largest was a 65-foot motor yacht that still was built at Algonac. Two years later, the Smiths sold Chris-Craft. The four brothers, Jay, Bernard, Owen, and Hamilton, were semi-retired, and Jay's son, Harson, had moved from CEO to chairman of the board. Harry H. Coll became the first president who was not a family member. Owen planned to sell his shares even

if the rest of the family retained theirs. The Smiths could see that boating's golden age was turning into a plastic age and that great and expensive manufacturing changes were needed to produce glass-reinforced plastic boats.

Fiberglass

The July 1959 issue of *Boats* magazine reported, "Public demand for glass reinforced plastic boats is here. This year at the various boat shows, about 40 percent were constructed with reinforced plastic. This figure represents an increase from 30 percent in 1958."

Plastic reinforced by fiberglass caused a revolution in boat building in the 1960s. Manufacturers called them fiberglass boats because plastic boats sounded faintly ridiculous—more likely to be used in a bathtub, perhaps, than in larger waters—and that is how we know them today. From the boatbuilders' viewpoint, the new material did not require skilled woodworkers, who were gradually disappearing, and it permitted easier construction of boats with fewer workers. The companies had to convert wood-building plants to fiberglass-building plants, which was a costly process that required the removal of the factory

A 1949 Chris-Craft Sportsman of 22 feet reflected the growing popularity of relatively small utilities. *Classic Boating*

machinery and installation of entirely different equipment. The companies could then produce boats that could be sold for less. Those who built at the most competitive levels could also trim their quality in ways that are much harder to see than shortcuts in wooden construction.

although the maintenance work for wood is more time consuming and expensive. The fiberglass revolution affected all of the large producers of wooden boats who lasted into the 1960s. After that, builders of wooden boats, like custom tailors, were hard to find and very expensive.

In 1962 Chris-Craft bought the Thompson Boat Company of New York. It was a small concern that manufactured two fiberglass outboard hulls and a 20-foot inboard hull available in both open and cruiser models. These boats became the first fiberglass Chris-Crafts and the first Chris-Craft boats to have inboard-outboard drives. The transition to fiberglass had begun.

In the early 1970s, Chris-Craft began a descending spiral of takeovers and reorganizations and was stripped of as much money as possible. When everything else was gone, it became one trade name used less often than some other names owned by a large manufacturer of fiberglass boats. When that manufacturer failed, the Chris-Craft name was bought by a British company that, at this writing, hopes to reestablish its fame.

Hacker

John L. Hacker—"The Dean of Yacht Designers" according to a *Motor Boating* article in 1959—was no longer a member of the company that bore his name, although he continued to design boats for them. During World War II, the company produced 34-foot radio-controlled boats for the navy from one of Hacker's designs. The boats were used to tow targets for gunnery practice. Other wartime craft made by the company were not Hacker's, but he became chief architect of the Eddy Boat Company, who also built military boats. While working there, he took over the plans for an air-sea rescue boat and redesigned the bottom to improve performance. After the war, Hacker worked for the Kehrig Manufacturing Company for a while and established a line of steel cruisers.

The relatively small Hacker Boat Company moved from government construction for World War II to construction for the Korean War. Other builders that had dealt with government red tape during World War II avoided Korean War construction. The Hacker Boat Company continued to build a few Hacker-designed pleasure boats on the side. As the end of the Korean War approached, the government canceled its contract and left the company without government support. It was burdened with a large supply of materials bought to build naval craft. The company was apparently desperate for a market and, for a time, built plywood outboard boats in addition to mahogany runabouts and utilities. Its sales became smaller and smaller. In the mid-1950s it cut its final connection

From the point of view of the purchasers, fiberglass boats were far easier to maintain than wooden boats and were usually less expensive. A good boat made of wood, properly maintained, could have as long and satisfactory a life as a good boat made of fiberglass, also properly maintained,

with Hacker and turned to another naval architect to build a few unattractive models before it closed its doors in 1957.

John L. Hacker remained involved with boats long after Christopher Columbus Smith died and Gar Wood turned away. He continued to design custom boats and established his own separate office and advertised as the John L. Hacker Co.

The Largest Runabout

One of Hacker's most striking designs was a 48-foot runabout, the largest one ever made. The boat was constructed in 1947 and 1948 by Hutchinson in Alexandria Bay, New York, on the upper St. Lawrence, for railroad magnate Charles P. Lyon. Her power was provided by a Packard V-12 that gave her a cruising speed of 50 miles per hour. Lyon named her *Pardon Me.* It has been suggested that this was an apology for the way she monopolized channel and harbor space. The boat had a series of owners, and one of them, Jim Lewis, bought her to be displayed at the Antique Boat Museum in Clayton, New York, where she is today.

The pilot model of Chris-Craft's Sea Skiff, built in Holland, Michigan, in 1953. It was a 22-foot lapstrake boat to compete with Lyman. *Classic Boating*

Postwar Racers

A 1949 advertisement showed a picture of the racing boat *My Sweetie* and said, "Winner of Gold Cup, Silver Cup, National Sweepstakes, and Presidents Cup. Designed, lofted, and supervised by John L. Hacker, NA. Four improved units will be available for 1950. A potential winner for you." *My Sweetie* was followed by the even more powerful *Miss Pepsi.* Both were stepped hydroplanes that successfully competed against the newer three-point hydroplanes. Hacker's old company wasn't interested in building racing boats, so he went to Les

Staudacher in Bay City. Staudacher had built some cruisers for Hacker, and Hacker launched him on a career of building racing boats, where he became modestly famous.

Miss Pepsi had a two-column article in the September 10, 1956, issue of *Time* magazine. Referring to the three-point racing boats that ran against *Pepsi,* the article said they "are designed to skim the surface, bouncing along on three small hunks of hull. Air flows under their almost flat bellies, and the boats try their best to take off. Almost any bump can send them soaring ... In contrast to the precarious ride of the other boats, *Miss Pepsi* displaces water like a Sunday speedboat, is kicked along by two 1,500-h.p. Allison aircraft engines, and throws a rough wake that is awesome indeed."

Miss Pepsi was the last conventional racer to win in the unlimited category. Horace Dodge Jr. had Hacker design two more boats that were to be bigger and better versions of *Miss Pepsi,* but Dodge's mother controlled the family purse strings. She disapproved of the divorce he sought at the time and wouldn't release money to build the boats. Dodge—described in the *Time* article as a "roly-poly playboy"— was becoming an alcoholic and was losing much of his drive. The new stepped hydroplanes were never built, and the three-point craft soon became the accepted racers.

Air-Sea Rescue Boat

Although Hacker continued to be best known for his runabouts, their day had largely passed. Even after he was no longer tied to his old company, he designed some runabouts for the Gage Marine Corporation of Lake Geneva, Wisconsin. Much of Hacker's time after the war was spent designing cruisers, and he was especially proud of these boats. Probably the highlight of his career was the design of a 94-foot, air-sea rescue boat for the U.S. Air Force in 1951. He worked until late February 1961, when he suffered a stroke. John L. Hacker died in early March 1961 at the age of 84. He had designed over a thousand boats. Joseph Gribbins wrote in *Nautical Quarterly,* "John Hacker died in early 1961, two years after Chris-Craft launched its first fiberglass speedboat, and four years before Century built its last mahogany runabout. His long life had almost exactly spanned the age of the mahogany runabout, a phenomenon whose elan and performance he had shaped and refined more than any other man."

Richardson

In February 1937, G. Reid Richardson, founder, chief executive, treasurer, and general manager, died. The company drifted into World War II production without him and acquired new owners and managers.

The Cobra, Chris-Craft's 1955 venture into plastic, which composed the hatch covers and tail fin for both 18- and 21-footers. Chris Smith, grandson of Christopher Columbus Smith, the company founder, drives this restored 18-footer. Twitchy handling and unfashionable streamlining limited the boat's popularity. *Classic Boating*

William Lindquist, the Richardson historian, has traced the concern's downward spiral. When the eventual postwar boat went into production, the hull was built by a Grand Rapids company that had wide experience in building molded plywood items that ranged from canoes to truck bodies but that could only mold large hulls in sections. The sections went to Richardson in North Tonawanda for assembly. The first new Richardson was a 25-footer that appeared in 1945. It was followed by a 34-foot V-bottom model in 1947. The new Richardson boats did not handle well and the laminates began to separate. During what should have been a postwar sales boom, employees were laid off, which caused a lot of dissatisfaction. One disgruntled former worker stole a company payroll at gunpoint. In

1948 Richardson went back to building its prewar 31-footer in the traditional planks-on-frame manner. In 1947 and 1949, strikes disturbed operations. There was a management reshuffle in 1948, and in 1950 the company brought out five models, including the 31-footer. Sales increased during the 1950s, and the largest boats Richardson made grew from 35 feet in 1950 to 46 feet in 1959.

Beginning in 1955, the factory was jammed with orders. The company seemed prosperous, although in view of later happenings, there surely were hidden problems.

Company officers looked for more capacity, perhaps for a new infusion of cash, and associated themselves with the Colonial Boat Works in Millville, New Jersey. In 1958 Colonial built the 35-foot Richardsons. The two companies

A 26-foot Chris-Craft Sea Skiff cruiser of 1957. *Chris-Craft Collection, Mariners' Museum, Newport News, Virginia*

were joined in 1959 under the name United Marine. Complaints began about the quality of the boats shipped to dealers and the slow payments to suppliers.

In 1960 United Marine contracted Avro, a Canadian aircraft company, to build aluminum hulls for the Richardson Division. This appeared to be a good move for both concerns. However, Richardson's value to Avro became questionable when Richardson, deeply in debt, discharged most of its workers and almost closed its plant. Harvey Smith, president of Avro, stepped in as United Marine collapsed and took over the presidency of Richardson.

Richardson and Avro completed about 150 aluminum boats. Some had problems, but Richardson was no longer strong enough to hold on until the difficulties were worked out. The construction costs of the aluminum boats were high, and again Richardson was unable to wait until that problem was solved. Avro, which propped up Richardson,

was in shaky financial condition itself and was taken over by Dehaviland. Richardson went bankrupt in 1962.

Matthews

The Matthews Company, one of the longest established cruiser builders, outlived Richardson. After the war, Matthews built pleasure craft and at first only produced the 38-footer, one of its most popular models. In 1949 the company widened the line to include a 32-footer and a 40-footer. The designers had not gone to extremes with the then-fashionable streamlining before the war, and their boats now looked crisp and up-to-date.

The company that had once adjusted easily to market conditions did not adjust well to postwar conditions. A great burst of interest in boating began after the war, but Matthews failed to meet it, as Edna Johnson, the Matthews historian, has pointed out. The company was stodgy in its sales efforts. It did not update factory machinery or methods and made little attempt to analyze costs.

Scott J. Matthews had turned management over to his son Carl by the company's 60th anniversary in 1950, although he still exercised control when he wanted to. Scott died in 1956, and by then Carl was mainly interested in airplanes. Carl left the running of the boat plant to a manager. Sales dwindled, and in 1958 the company built 52 boats. In 1963 the company built 25. The plant dated back to before 1918 and was aging, as were those who owned it. The Matthews family—two sons and two daughters—were close to retirement age and eventually decided that they should sell.

Change of Owners

In October 1964 Charles Hutchinson of Cleveland bought the Matthews company. Some of its longtime workers left at that time and were "afraid that the management was not stable," as one put it. Before the sale, Matthews had built everything that went into the boats, even the upholstery. Hutchinson closed some of the shops and bought everything possible from outside suppliers, including fiberglass hulls from Halmatic in England. In a full-page advertisement in January 1969, the company announced, "Worth Waiting For: Matthews Fiberglass 45." This wording perhaps admitted the company had waited too long before it changed to the new material. During 1965 to 1970, the company built five wood 60-footers. For a year, Matthews produced both wood and fiberglass 45s, so called even though the fiberglass hulls were 45 feet, 7 inches long. Matthews then dropped the wooden boats and called the fiberglass ones 46s. The company made its own mold for a 56-foot fiberglass boat in 1971 and built a stretched version of the older wooden 53-footer to use as a "plug" for the mold. The wooden 56-footer was later sold and at this writing still exists.

In the 1970s Matthews built trawlers—pleasure cruisers that moved at 7 or 8 knots and emphasized seagoing qualities rather than speed, which had become fashionable, helped in part by the fuel shortages of the 1970s. Matthews was behind its competitors in producing these models, even though its trawler hulls were identical to those of its faster boats. They just had slower engines.

By the 1970s the 46-footers were the smallest boats Matthews built. The company had once made 32- and 38-footers, which were much more suitable for family use and maintenance, and more of what was now wanted in the market. Yet Matthews produced none of the smaller sizes at that time. Sales shrank continuously. As the company sold fewer boats, it could not raise wages to contemporary levels, and workers became increasingly unhappy. In the early 1970s suppliers began to demand cash on delivery.

Splish Splash, a 23-foot 1956 Chris-Craft, shows the angular design favored then. It was the antithesis of streamlining. The boat has its original Hercules six-cylinder engine and the Chris-O-Matic transmission, an early and temperamental automatic that has held up in this boat. *Classic Boating*

Matthews turned to fiberglass too late, and it made the wrong size of boats. Bad record keeping may have contributed to its failure. It never had the careful cost accounting that typified Chris-Craft. Matthews built only seven boats in 1974 and closed its doors that December. It agreed to receivership the following January.

Lyman

After World War II, Lyman and Century built relatively small craft and provided similar markets with very different boats.

From 1957 through 1959, Chris-Craft built 92 Silver Arrows. These 19-foot boats had reinforced fiberglass decks and sides of fiberglass-covered spruce. The double-planked bottoms were uncoated. The maximum speed was 42 miles per hour. Styling reflects tail-finned autos of the day. *Classic Boating*

Lyman—whose utility models and lapstrake planking were widely copied—emerged from World War II and went back into production of white-painted, round-bilged lapstrake open boats. Lyman's Golden Age soon followed. At first, it made more outboard motorboats than inboards, but the inboard boats gradually caught up. To keep assembly line construction running smoothly, Lyman kept the number of models low and only built six different kinds of boats. "Utility," the name the company originated, had lost its distinction, so Lyman used "runabout," as did the others, although few of anyone's products were now in the classic runabout form.

Before the war, Bill Lyman experimented with planks made of marine plywood and found they held up better and were more uniform than plain wood planking. As the plant came out of the war, it settled down and made properly shaped planks of uniform quality that were cut from five-ply marine plywood. They used these planks to make Lyman pleasure boats. While the boats passed along one of two assembly lines (a line for outboards, a line for inboards), the necessary parts and tools waited at either side of the line.

Lyman only had a few master builders after the war. Some had scattered, and old age had removed many. The

A post–World War II Hacker stock 26-foot runabout built by the Hacker Boat Company. Hacker still designed boats for his old company although he no longer owned it. The company continued to offer classic runabouts but sold few. *Gerald Farber*

remaining builders put together the first sample of each model. As each piece of wood was shaped to fit the hull and before it was fastened into place, they built the necessary pattern or jig that the less-skilled workers would use to make those pieces on the assembly line with their electric hand tools. One description of the plant said that at 7 A.M., 200 people started work, and there rose ear-rattling sounds of drills, planers, saws, shapers, and other machinery.

Bill Lyman died in the summer of 1952. Fred E. Wiehn, who had been vice president and general manager, continued to run things smoothly. Unlike many other companies, Lyman continued energetically after the founding family died out. The plant produced 75 boats a week and shipped them to a waiting market that was fed by 225 dealers.

In 1954 Chris-Craft awakened to this market and set up a plant to produce nothing but round-bottom lapstrake boats. Other builders also entered the lapstrake market, although Chris-Craft was Lyman's most important competitor.

Lyman remained healthy and built 5,000 boats in 1958, its peak year. A 28-foot cruiser was added to the line in 1960, probably in response to Chris-Craft's lapstrake cruisers. Inboard-outboard engines were installed in some of the larger boats in 1963, but by the late 1960s, lapstrake sales shrunk for both Lyman and Chris-Craft.

Fiberglass boats cut into the market. The difficulty of translating Lyman individuality into fiberglass may have discouraged changes. In the late 1960s, the Lyman plant had to be closed periodically, was sold, sold again, and then resold. Some owners wrung as much money out of the company as possible. Finally, in the 1970s a brave new owner determined to start fiberglass construction used a Lyman lapstrake wooden boat as the "plug" around which the mold was built. The company produced some lapstrake-looking fiberglass Lymans, but it was too late. Other builders who had converted earlier had too much momentum, and when even the well-established fiberglass producers faced hard times in the 1980s, Lyman disappeared.

Century

Century restarted pleasure boat construction in 1945 and began with its prewar models. The demand for inboard boats was so great that in 1946 Century leased a building in Chattanooga, Tennessee, and installed a plant there to produce most of the outboard models. That left more room to build inboards at their main factory. By 1947 Century at Manistee turned out five new inboard models with 32 optional arrangements.

Changes came quickly. In 1948 and 1949, Overlakes Freight Corporation became the owner. Overlakes owned 12 auto-carrying vessels on the Great Lakes, hence the

Pardon Me, completed in 1948, is considered the largest runabout ever built at 48 feet in length. Designed by Hacker and built by Hutchinson, she is powered by a 1,500-horsepower Packard V-12 engine. *Antique Boat Museum*

name. The Chattanooga plant was closed in 1950, and the outboard construction returned to Manistee.

The company introduced the 19-foot Viking (actually 18 feet, 3 inches) in 1953. It was an inboard white-painted lapstrake utility that looked like it had come straight from Lyman's factory. As the Century historians, Paul, Frank, and Trudi Miklos, have said, it was "a poorly disguised copy of Lyman's top-selling inboard, the 18-foot Islander." Because of the growing popularity of clinker-built boats, the plant was inundated with orders for it.

The Sea Maid of 1954 was the last of a long line of carvel-built mahogany boats of that name. It is a handsome boat in traditional style and is a collectors' item today. Competitors Gar Wood and Dodge had dropped away, and Hackercraft had dwindled almost to nothing, which provided

My Sweetie, a winning Hacker racing boat of 1949, sported Hacker's autograph. *Marion Hacker Hurst*

Miss Pepsi, the last of the winning stepped hydroplane unlimited racers, was designed by Hacker and built in 1950 by Staudacher of Bay City, Michigan. Today, the boat resides in the Dossin Great Lakes Museum. *Dossin Great Lakes Museum, Detroit*

an opportunity for greater Century sales. Richard Arbib, an auto stylist, was commissioned to design a new 20-foot Coronado, a boat with a mahogany hull picked out in white, a white transom, and a sleek removable plastic top amidships. She was largely an open boat, with the engine—Gray, Chrysler, Cadillac, or Norberg—under a box in the middle, following the pattern made popular by Lyman's utilities (but no one even whispered the name *utility*). One of the first boats was shipped to Florida in 1953 and was entered in the Around Miami Beach Marathon. It won and set a new record.

Sales manager Bob Lutz managed to have Centuries play parts in movies. Centuries appeared in *You Can't Run Away From It* with June Allyson and Jack Lemmon; in another movie with Tyrone Power; and in *On Golden Pond* with Katharine Hepburn and Henry Fonda. The singer Peggy Lee posed with a Century. Every effort was made to tie the boat to popular figures and popular interests of the day.

The company worked closely with the American Water Ski Association and provided emblems for skiers who jumped 100 feet or more—members of the Century Club. Fred Wiley, an area sales manager for Century, became a well-known figure at water ski tournaments and was always ready to give a tow with his Century for a practice run. He was also the driver when every water ski record was made during his active years. When he died in March 1963, the Water Ski Association established a trophy in his name to be given annually to the best driver in the National Water Ski Championships. Century continued to be their boat of choice.

Fiberglass Emphasis

In 1969 Allan Hegg, an engineer with considerable experience, became the fifth owner of Century. During the 1970s he pushed fiberglass construction, temporarily brought in men who were experts in that field, and reorganized and expanded the Manistee plant. He wanted frequent new models and liked boats that had inboard/outboard engine installations. Hegg overhauled the dealer network to improve sales.

Sales of pleasure boats plunged in 1980 and Century lost $9 million in sales, but as the recession eased, Century moved into the black again in 1984. The Century catalog for 1984 shows the company at its height and offered a variety of boats—all fiberglass—from cruisers under 30 feet to a "Tournament Skier" designed especially for that sport. The Coronado had two interior arrangements, and a variety of small, fast boats—down to the "Resorter 18"—were also offered. None of the boats followed what, before World War II, had become the traditional runabout pattern of separate cockpits, full-width decks, and engines under hatches. Except for the pocket cruisers, all the boats were utilities, although that term was never used. It was seldom mentioned again by any builder of small fiberglass open boats, which almost invariably were called runabouts.

Hegg decided he could cut expenses and set up a factory in Florida, but apparently the Florida operation was a heavy drain on the treasury. In 1986 he sold the company to a new owner who would supposedly inject the money needed to carry it through. Instead, payroll checks bounced, and in November 1986 the banks foreclosed. The downward slide continued until Yamaha bought what was left. It now produces a full line of its own fiberglass Centuries in Florida that are powered by Yamaha outboard motors. The company that first made its name as a builder of outboard motorboats has returned to that product.

An enthusiast has bought some old names and molds, the Coronado and Resorter, and now produces those boats in small numbers. Fiberglass craft have been produced for so long that good early models have their own nostalgic appeal.

After World War II, Hacker mainly designed cruisers. *Sirocco* has the typical Hacker hull with tumblehome aft and flare forward. *Hacker Collection, Mariners' Museum, Newport News, Virginia*

Heather is a 41-foot Matthews Convertible Sedan from 1954. The boat could be converted to a sport model by folding away the hinged partition that separated the deckhouse from the cockpit. The flying bridge is a later addition. *Classic Boating*

Growing Companies
Burger

During World War II, Burger was still able to build sizable wooden vessels. It produced, among many other craft, wooden minesweepers that would not trigger the magnetic fuses of mines. In 1951 the Navy ordered seven more wooden minesweepers for the Korean War.

The following year the company—which had built wooden pleasure cruisers, welded steel commercial fishing tugs, and a few welded steel pleasure boats before the war—began a line of welded steel cruisers that ranged from 53 to 80 feet in length. It worked with Reynolds Aluminum, and produced the 36-foot welded aluminum cruiser *Virginia* for Reynolds in 1952.

In the mid-1960s, Burger stopped producing stock welded steel boats and specialized in custom-built aluminum cruisers from 70 to 125 feet. It continued successfully until the 1980s when Henry E. Burger became ill. He had no successors in the family, so he sold the company, which had a full two-year order book, to John G. McMillian. McMillian decided to relocate the company to Florida. The workforce wanted to stay in Manitowoc, and

A 1959 Lyman 19-foot Inboard Runabout. (After World War II, Lyman switched from calling its boats "utilities" to "runabouts".) *Classic Boating*

skilled workers in aluminum were hard to find elsewhere. The workers dug in their heels, and a disgusted McMillian sold the company to Tacoma Boatbuilding in Tacoma, Washington. Tacoma failed, and Burger was ordered to close in November 1990.

After 15 months of legal struggles, David Ross and Jim Ruffolo reopened the company in Manitowoc in February 1993. Since then, Burger has produced custom welded aluminum cruisers from 76 to 118 feet. The boats have a modern look, but they also look seagoing. They do not have the extreme swoops and bulges that make some current cruisers look like Italian sport cars on steroids, as one yachting magazine said.

Tiara

While many boatbuilders were on a downward course, Leon Slikkers moved in the opposite direction. Slikkers, born on a Michigan farm and educated up to the ninth grade, was a foreman at the Chris-Craft plant in Holland, Michigan. He loved working with wood and built a 14-foot runabout in his garage after work. At that time,

Chris-Craft had begun to experiment with fiberglass and made it into a few very small parts with compound shapes in hopes to reduce labor costs.

Slikkers was an expert woodworker who had the foresight to become an expert in fiberglass. During a Chris-Craft strike in the early 1950s, he decided to start off on his own. He sold his home and started a company he called Slickcraft. His family lived above the boat-building shop. In 1956 he began to experiment and covered a plywood hull with fiberglass. Another local company began to make basic fiberglass hulls that looked transparent and did not have what now are the standard gelcoat exteriors. They wanted someone to finish them, so Slickcraft took the hulls, fixed any air bubbles, and sanded, primed, and painted the hulls. In 1957 Slickcraft took 5 to 10 hulls, finished them, and installed mahogany decks. The supplier began to make fiberglass decks that simulated wooden planking, and Slickcraft added narrow white-painted stripes between the simulated planks.

In late 1958 Slikkers contracted another firm to supply hulls and decks that were already gelcoated in color. Slikkers used his own designs and provided the wood plugs used to form the molds. The next year he felt he had learned enough and began his own fiberglass construction. He had pioneered fiberglass, and Slickcraft was on its way to success.

In 1962 Slikkers moved his shop into an old skating rink in Holland. Two years later he produced a deep V-bottom, trailerable boat with a cuddy cabin that he called SS235. It immediately tapped a new market and turned out to be Slickcraft's most popular product. In 1966 he built a larger plant in Holland. At that time, Century was a much bigger

Mahogany Rose, an 18-foot 1951 Sea Maid, was powered by a Gray Fireball engine. Sea Maids were introduced in 1930 and ended production in 1954. *Classic Boating*

Century competed with Lyman's lap-strake boats. The *Raven*, introduced in 1957, was a mahogany-planked lap-strake boat painted black. *Never Again* is a husky 1963 22-footer. Production ended in 1967 due to growing fiberglass competition. *Classic Boating*

Koch Machine (the owner's name is Koch, pronounced "Coke") is a 1966 Century Sabre 18 that blended mahogany and fiberglass. The boat was designed by auto stylist Richard Arbib. The windshield is plexiglass, and the white side decks and the shelter cabin are fiberglass. The foredeck is vinyl-covered plywood. The hull was built of mahogany over white oak frames. Sabre 18s had various engines that provided speeds of up to 60 miles per hour. In 1967 production of the Sabre ended and was replaced by all-fiberglass craft. *Classic Boating*

As other boatbuilders faded, Tiara grew and developed fiberglass boats in Holland, Michigan, where a Chris-Craft plant once flourished. The Tiara 3800 Open, a present-day product of Holland, contrasts strikingly with early cruisers. Tiaras range from 29 to 52 feet. Two diesel engines drive this 38-footer. Its hull has integrated longitudinal composite wood stringers and was built of hand-laid fiberglass with a gelcoat exterior. *Tiara Yachts*

company than Slickcraft, but the latter now had a unique experience in fiberglass boat building. Century drew on Slikkers' fiberglass knowledge in setting up its own fiberglass line. Slikkers actually built 50 of their first 17-foot fiberglass hulls.

In 1969 Slikkers sold Slickcraft to a New York company but remained as president. After what he calls "a good learning experience," he resigned in 1973 and started on his own again. He established S2 Yachts, Inc. and made sailboats. S2 stood for "Slikkers, Second Time." In 1977 he returned to powered craft and manufactured Pursuit sport fishing boats. Two years later, he doubled his plant capacity and introduced Tiara Yachts—sizable fiberglass cruisers. Today, Tiara operates plants in Holland,

Michigan, its headquarters, and in Swansboro, North Carolina. Its founder's early recognition of fiberglass as the future hull material led his company to vigorous growth as the older, established boatbuilders gradually faded from the scene.

A Century Tournament Skier, a 21-foot, 1-inch fiberglass boat from 1984. That was probably the company's most successful year of the fiberglass era. *From the 1984 Century Catalog*

BIBLIOGRAPHY

Books

Arndt, Leslie E. *The Bay County Story*. Bay City, Michigan: Bay City Times, 1982. [Boatbuilders of Bay City]

Barrett, J. Lee. *Speed Boat Kings*. Detroit: Arnold Powers, 1939. Reprint for Historical Society of Michigan, Berrien Springs, Michigan: Hardscrabble Books, 1989.

Barry, James P. *Hackercraft*. St. Paul, Minnesota: MBI Publishing Company, 2002.

Burridge, George Nau. *Green Bay Workhorses: The Nau Tug Line*. Manitowoc, Wisconsin: The Manitowoc Maritime Museum, 1991.

Day, Thomas Fleming. *The Voyage of Detroit*. 1912. Reprint, Atlantic Beach, North Carolina: Eastern Offset Publishing Co., 1997.

Dodington, Fossey, Gockel, Ogilvie, and Smith. *The Greatest Little Motor Boat Afloat*. Toronto: Stoddart, Boston Mills Press, 1994. [Disappearing Propeller Boats]

Duke, A. H., and W. M. Gray. *The Boatbuilders of Muskoka*. Toronto: Stoddart, Boston Mills Press, 1985.

Duncan, Robert Bruce. *Cutwater: Speedboats and Launches from the Golden Age of Boating*. Novato, California: Top Ten Publishing, 1993.

du Plessis, Hugo. *Fibreglass Boats*., 3d ed. London: A. & C. Black, Adlard Coles Nautical, 1996.

Durham, Bill, ed. *Steamboats and Modern Steam Launches*. Portland, Oregon: Boat House, 1997. [A volume reprinting all issues of the magazine of the same name. Includes naptha information.]

Farmer, Weston. *From My Old Boat Shop*. 1979. Reprint, Portland, Oregon: Boat House, 1996.

Fostle, D. W. *Speedboat*. Mystic, Connecticut: Mystic Seaport Museum Stores, 1988.

Gérald Guétat. *Classic Speedboats, 1916–1939*. Osceola, Wisconsin: Motorbooks International, 1997.

Gray, William M., and Timothy C. Du Vernet. *Wood & Glory*. Toronto: Stoddart, Boston Mills Press, 1997. [Muskoka Boats]

Grayson, Stan. *Old Marine Engines*. Camden, Maine: International Marine Publishing Company, 1982. [Contains Lozier history not in later editions]

————. *Old Marine Engines*. 3d ed. Marblehead, Massachusetts: Devereaux Books, 1998.

————. *Engines Afloat*. 2 vols. Marblehead, Massachusetts: Devereaux Books, 1999.

Gribbins, Joseph. *Chris-Craft: A History*. Marblehead, Massachusetts: Devereaux Books, 2001.

Hunn, Peter. *The Old Outboard Book*. Rev. ed. Camden, Maine: McGraw-Hill, International Marine, 1994.

Hunt, C. W. *Booze, Boats and Billions*. Toronto: McClelland and Stewart, 1988.

Keats, John. *The Skiff and the River*. Nantucket, Massachusetts: Herrick Collection, 1988. [St. Lawrence Skiffs]

Kunhardt, C. P. *Steam Yachts and Launches: Their Machinery and Management*. New York: Forest and Stream Publishing Company, 1891.

Lindquist, William C. *The Richardson Story*. Ontario, New York: privately published, 1990.

Mansfield, J. B. *History of the Great Lakes*. 2 vols. 1899. Reprint, Cleveland, Ohio: Freshwater Press, 1972.

Martin, Fred W. *1901 Album of Designs for Boats, Launches and Yachts*. 1901. Reprint, Mount Prospect, Illinois: Altair Publishing Company, 1980.

McCulley, Douglas Garfield. *SeaBird: Muskoka's SeaBirds*. Port Carling, Ontario: Muskoka Lakes Museum, 1995.

Miklos, Paul, Frank Miklos, and Trudi Miklos. *Classic Century Powerboats*. St. Paul, Minnesota: MBI Publishing Company, 2002.

Mercier, Gilbert B. *Pleasure Yachts of the Thousand Islands*. Clayton, New York: The Shipyard Press, 1981.

Mollica, Anthony S., Jr. *Gar Wood Boats: Classics of a Golden Era*. Osceola, Wisconsin: MBI Publishing Company, 1999.

————. *The American Wooden Runabout*. St. Paul, Minnesota: MBI Publishing Company, 2002.

Mollica, Anthony Jr., and Jack Savage. *Chris-Craft Boats*. St. Paul, Minnesota: MBI Publishing Company, 2001.

Mollica, Tony. *Gar Wood Boats: Every One a Classic*. Syracuse, New York: privately published, n.d. [Pamphlet]

Moore, C. Philip. *Yachts in a Hurry*. New York: W.W. Norton & Company, 1993. [Contains the author's "Commuter Register" giving detail about the boats]

Neal, Robert J. *Packards at Speed*. Kent, Washington: Aero-Marine History Publishing Co., 1995.

————. *Master Motor Builders*. Kent, Washington: Aero-Marine History Publishing Co., 2000.

O'Brien, T. Michael. *Guardians of the Eighth Sea: A History of the U.S. Coast Guard on the Great Lakes*. Washington, D.C.: U.S. Coast Guard, 1976.

Pitrone, Jean Maddern, and Joan Potter Elwart. *The Dodges*. South Bend, Indiana: Icarus Press, 1981.

Rodengen, Jeffrey L. *Evenrude, Johnson and the Legend of OMC*. Ft. Lauderdale, Florida: Write Stuff Syndicate, 1993.

————. *The Legend of Chris-Craft*. 2d ed. Ft. Lauderdale, Florida: Write Stuff Syndicate, 1993.

Savage, Jack. *Chris-Craft*. Osceola, Wisconsin: MBI Publishing Company, 2000.

Speltz, Robert. *The Real Runabouts*. Vols. 1–3. Mason City, Iowa: privately published, 1977, 1978, 1980.

Wangard, Norm, and Jim Wangard. *Classic Powercraft*. Vols. 1 and 2. Colton, California: Classic Powercraft, Inc., 1986, 1987.

Watts, Peter, and Tracy Marsh. *W. Watts & Sons, Boat Builders*. Oshawa, Ontario: Mackinaw Productions, 1997.

Wendt, Gordon. *In the Wake of the "Walk-in-the-Water": the Marine History of Sandusky, Ohio*. Sandusky, Ohio: privately published, 1984.

Wilson, Harold. *Boats Unlimited*. Erin, Ontario: Boston Mills Press, 1990. [International racing by Muskoka-built boats]

Wittig, William G. *The Story of the Century*. Manistee, Michigan: The Century Boat Company, 1984.

Periodicals

Antique Boat Museum. *Gazette Annuals 1999–2002*, Clayton, New York.

"*Au Revoir*, a New Speed Launch on Detroit River." *Sail and Sweep*, November 1903.

"*Baby Gar IV* Wins Fisher-Allison Race." *Motor Boating*, October 1924. [Gar Wood's racing in white tie and tails]

Bailey, Walter F. "What Is an Ultra-Express Cruiser?" *Motor Boating*, October 1922.

————. "Introducing a New Cigarette." *Motor Boating*, August 1923.

"Boat Production Capacity Increased." *Motor Boating*, May 1930.

Bond, Hallie. "What Is 'Museum Quality?'" *Wooden Boat*, September/October 1998.

"Building Methods in a Modern Plant." *Motor Boating*, July 1930.

"The Burger Standard 36-footer for 1921." *Motor Boat*, 10 December 1920. [A full-page advertisement for the same boat is in *Motor Boat*, 25 December 1920.]

Brennan, Walter K. "John L. Hacker, Dean of Yacht Designers." *Motor Boating*, December 1959.

"Canadians Are Hosts to American Yachtsmen." *Motor Boating*, October 1922. [Fisher-Allison race where Wood's and Vincent's boats were disqualified]

Cecil, Owen. "Great Lakes Small Craft." *Wooden Boat*, July/August 1991.

Chapman, Charles F. "English Sportsmanship Wins." *Motor Boating*, October 1931. [Wood-Done contretemps during 1931 Harmsworth Trophy race]

"*Chriscraft* and *Rainbow* Tie for Gold Cup." *Motor Boating*, October 1922.

"Chris-Craft Announces Utility Boats." *Power Boating*, September 1932.

"Chris-Craft in Coast Guard Service." *Power Boating*, May 1930.

"Chris Smith, 1861–1939." *Motor Boat*, October 1939.

"Col. Hayward Makes Fisher-Allison Decision." *Motor Boating*, March 1923. [Disqualification of Wood and Vincent]

"Commuting: Express Cruiser vs. Railroad." *Motor Boating*, July 1924.

Crook, Melvin. "Why Jettison the Mechanic?" *Yachting*, January 1938.

"Cruisabouts for 1932." *Power Boating*, November 1931.

"The Cry for Production." *Motor Boating*, January 1930.

"The Development of an Idea." *Motor Boating*, May 1926.
Dodge, Horace E. "Mass Production for Boats." *Motor Boating*, February 1930.

Dodington, Paul, Joe Fossey, Paul Gockel, III, James Smith, and Peter H. Spectre, "The Greatest Little Motor Boat Afloat." *Wooden Boat*, November/December 1983. [Disappearing Propeller boats. Much like the book of the same name, but with Spectre's comments added.]

"Eastern Boats Win at Detroit." *Motor Boating*, October 1924.

Eastman, David. "Classic Cruisers." *Wooden Boat*, May/June 1978. [Richardson design]

Farmer, Weston. "Those Wonderful Naphtha Launches." *Yachting*, August 1973.

"A Fast One for Commuting." *Power Boating*, November 1931. [Hacker-designed and -built 40-foot torpedo runabout *Lockpat II*]

Fiest, Terry. "All About Cobras." *Classic Boating*, November/ December 1995.

"Finance and Boat Construction." *Motor Boating*, December 1923. [Reorganization of Great Lakes Boat Building Corp.]

Fischer, W. K. "Glass Reinforced Plastics." *Boats*, July 1959.

"Forty Years of Boat Building." *Motor Boating*, November 1930. [History of Matthews]

Fostle, D. W. "The Boatbuilders of Alexandria Bay." *Wooden Boat*, September/October 1982, November/December 1982.

"*Frances*, 104-Ft. Express Cruiser." *The Rudder*, January 1921.

"*Gar Jr.* Breaks Record." *The Rudder*, June 1921. [*Gar Jr. II* records on Atlantic and Hudson River]

"*Gar Jr. II* Explores Uncharted Waters." *Motor Boating*, September/October 1921.

Grant, C. L. "How *Mitt II* Won the Gold Cup." *Motor Boating*, September 1911.

———. "The A.P.B.A. Gold Cup Goes to Lake George." *Motor Boating,* September 1913.

Gribbins, Joseph. "Hacker and His Craft." *Nautical Quarterly,* summer 1981.

Gribbins, Joseph, and Jay Higgins. "Pushing the Limits: The Quest for Powerboat Speed." *Wooden Boat,* May/June 2000, July/August 2000.

"Hacker-Craft Features Utilities." *Motor Boat,* January 1939.

Hacker, John. "The Conventional Hydroplane." *Motor Boating,* April 1951. [An article paired with one by Ted Jones, "The Multiple Point Hydro," under the overall heading "It's All in the Bottom"]

Hacker, John L. "1922 *Fleetfoot,* a Fast Runabout." *Classic Boating,* September/October 1999. [Reprint of Hacker's instructions and plans for building a boat by amateurs]

"Hacker Runabouts and Cruisers." *Power Boating,* January 1938.

Herreshoff, L. Francis. "An Introduction to Yachting." *The Rudder,* August/September 1958. [Steam launches]

"How Fine Runabouts Are Built." *Motor Boating,* May 1929. [Hacker construction]

Huber, Bob. "Mr. Chris-Craft." *Classic Boating,* July/August 1994. [A. W. MacKerer]

———. "John Hacker Remembered." *Classic Boating,* July/August 1996. [Interview with Tom Flood]

———. "Chris Smith: A Lifetime in Boats." *Classic Boating,* November/December 1996. [Recollections of Chris Smith, grandson of the original Chris Smith]

———. "In Defense of Lyman." *Classic Boating,* May/June1998.

———. "Depression Era Boats." *Classic Boating,* September/October 1999.

Jones, Ted. "The Multiple Point Hydro." *Motor Boating,* April 1951. [Paired with article by John Hacker, *q.v.*]

"Kingfisher—A New Express Cruiser," *Motor Boat,* 25 October 1916.

"Larger Speed Tender Is Kermath Powered." *Power Boating,* November 1931.

"The Lyman Story." *Motor Boat,* May 1951.

"Lyman Tenders and Runabouts." *Power Boating,* August 1934. [Photo page of various models]

Magnusson, Craig. "Chris-Craft by the Numbers." *ACBS Rudder,* winter 2000. [This is the quarterly journal of the Antique & Classic Boat Society, not the venerable but now defunct boating monthly.]

"The Mail Must Go Through." *Power Boating,* August 1936.

"*Marguerite II*—40-foot Military Cruiser." *Motor Boat,* 25 September 1916.

"A Matthews 46 Sport Fisherman." *Power Boating,* September 1932.

Matthews, Scott J. "Development of the Motor Yacht." *Motor Boating,* December 1913. [Installation of trolling engine]

Menkel, Tom. "Gold Cup Shades of the Past." *Motor Boating,* August 1934.

Millar, Gordon H. "The Heritage of Early Marine Engines." *Classic Boating,* May/June 1995.

"*Miss Liberty II,* of Buffalo." *Motor Boat,* 25 November 1920.

Mocksfield, Wayne. "*Godfather,* Standard 26' Chris-Craft." *Classic Boating,* November/December 1999.

"Modern Merchandising of Motor Boats." *Motor Boating,* March 1927.

"Monster Boat Plant Opens." *Motor Boating,* May 1930. [Dodge plant at Newport News]

"More People Than Ever Are Buying Boats." *Power Boating,* December 1935. [Chris-Craft, Robinson]

Morris, Everett B. "New Luster for the Old Gold Cup." *Yachting*, October 1937.

"Motor Boat's Mates." *Motor Boat,* 10 April 1929. [Brief histories of boat builders, engine builders, and other companies producing maritime products]

Mowle, Kevin. "The Model T Boat." *Old Autos,* 5 May 1997. [Gildeyford boats]

Myers, Robert G. "They Built a Reputation on Lapstrake Hulls." *Motor Boating*, January 1950. [Lyman]

"The New Cadet," *Motor Boating*, June 1927. [Describes Chris-Craft mass production]

"New Cruiser by Gar Wood." *Power Boating*, February 1935. [26-foot stock boat]

"New Models for 1932." *Power Boating*, November 1931. [Matthews]

"New Richardson Utility Boat." *Power Boating*, June 1932. [John Hacker's *Mary K.*]

"A New Super-Speed Cruiser." *Motor Boat,* 25 December 1920.

Nock, Frederick S. "The Trend in Motor Boat Design." *Motor Boating*, December 1912.

Nutting, William Washburn. "The Development of Motor Boat Types." *Motor Boating,* December 1910.

———. "The Express Cruiser." *Motor Boat,* 10 December 1916.

"*Nymph II.*" *Motor Boat,* 10 March 1929. [Robinson boat designed by Hacker]

"The 104-footer *Frances,* Largest Express Power Cruiser." *Yachting*, January 1921.

"*Pam*—An Unusual 62-footer." *Yachting*, January 1922.

Power, Robert E. "Where Great Lakes Craft Come From." *Power Boating*, June 1916. [Great Lakes Boat Building Corp.]

"Power Boat to Attempt the Western Ocean Passage on a Voyage from Detroit to St. Petersburg, Russia." *The Rudder,* June 1912. [*Detroit* by Matthews. Includes plans.]

Price, Ben K. "Horace Dodge Wins Gold Cup." *Power Boating,* September 1932.

"Production Methods in Motor Boat Building." *Motor Boating*, May 1925.

"A Progressive Boat Plant." *Motor Boating,* April 1930. [Robinson]

"Quarter-Deck Talk." *The Rudder,* December 1900.

Reis, George. "Behind the Scenes with Gar Wood." *Motor Boating*, February 1935.

Robinson, John G. "America Keeps British Trophy by Technicality." *Power Boating,* October 1931.

———. "*Miss America X*, a Super Hydro." *Power Boating,* September 1932.

———. "Evolution of the Runabout." *Motor Boating,* January 1940.

"Robinson Marine Construction Busy." *Power Boating,* July 1936.

"Robinson to Specialize in Custom Built Craft." *Motor Boating,* February 1933.

Rudolph, Bruce. "Senator W. E. Sanford and His Yacht *NAIAD.*" *Freshwater* [Marine Museum of the Great Lakes at Kingston], spring 1997.

Sabine, Lillian. "Miss Marion Barbara Carstairs." *Motor Boating,* October 1929.

"*Salome,* Henry Ringling's New Express Cruiser." *Motor Boat,* 25 November 1916.

Schlegel, John E. "Evolution of the 60-Foot Motor Yacht," *Motor Boat,* December 25, 1916.

"Seagull." *Lakeland Boating,* March 1983.

"The Seagull Commuting Cruisers." *Motor Boating*, February 1930.

Shield, Harold D. "Minett and Minett-Shields." *Wooden Boat*, January/February 1994.

———. "Bryson Shields." *Power Boating Canada*, vol. 15, no. 2. [The magazine is undated; it was published in the spring of 2000.]

"A 62-foot Combination Cruiser and Day Boat." *Yachting*, December 1920.

"A 65-foot Cruiser Designed by the Defoe Boat and Motor Works," *Motor Boat,* 10 December 1916.

Slauson, Harold Whiting. "How *Dixie II* Defended the Gold Cup." *Motor Boating*, September 1909.

———. "The Era of the Stock Motor Boat," *Motor Boating*, April 1912.

———. "Racing for the Gold Cup." *Motor Boating*, September 1912.

Slauson, Kinsley Wilcox. "Winning the Gold Cup for Frontenac." *Motor Boating*, September 1910.

Spectre, Peter H. "The Lyman Legend." *Wooden Boat*, May/June 1988.

"*Spray V*, 50-foot Passenger Boat of the Thousand Islands." *Motor Boat,* 10 October 1920.

Strawbridge, James B. "The Cruise of Betty." *The Rudder,* July 1902.

Sutton, George W., Jr. "Dashing to Work." *Motor Boating*, February 1929.

———. "Through Spray to Business." *Motor Boating*, February 1930.

"*Suzanne*—76-foot High-Speed Cruiser." *Motor Boat,* 10 November 1916.

"*Sylvan, Jr.*" *Motor Boat*, 10 September 1914.

"Tarnished Gold Cup." *Time,* 10 September 1956. [Favorable description of *Miss Pepsi* vs. three-point racers]

Thompson, Clay. "Robinson Seagull Cruiser." *Classic Boating*, January/February 2002.

Wallin, Mel. "Something New in Remote Control." *The Rudder,* June 1924.

Wangard, Jim. "Industrial Designer Fred Hudson." *Classic Boating*, September/October 1998.

———. "Koch Machine." *Classic Boating*, January/February 1999.

———. "*Jay-Dee II*: 26' Special Race Boat." *Classic Boating,* March/April 1999.

———. "Dodge Water Car." *Classic Boating*, September/October 2001.

———. "The Legacy of *Thunderbird*." *Classic Boating.,* November/December 2002.

Warnes, Kathleen. "Rumrunning on the Detroit River." *Inland Seas*, 1997.

Weisenburger, Gary. "Lyman: A Sleeping Assembly Line." *Wooden Boat*, May/June 1988.

"Where Lozier Motors Are Made." *The Rudder,* August 1900.

"Where Speed Is Worth While." *Motor Boating*, May 1929. [Robinson]

Whitaker, Morris M. "The Problem of Cruiser Design." *Motor Boating*, December 1913.

Wren, Sally-Ann, and Patrick Wren. "Muskoka." Antique Boat Museum *Gazette Annual 2000.*

Zipperer, Sandra. "Kahlenberg Brothers Company of Two Rivers, Wisconsin, 1895 to the Present." *Anchor News,* Wisconsin Maritime Museum, April/May/June 1998.

Published Scrapbooks

(Key articles in these scrapbooks are also listed above under Periodicals.)

Definitive collections by Campbell of old articles about racing boats.

Collection by Milkovich of contemporary material on *Cigarette*.

Informal Company Histories

Burger Boat Company, "Burger History."

Tiara Yachts, "A Historical Perspective."

Videos

Chris-Craft black-and-white silent promotional film of 1929 [transferred to video].

Lyman, Legend of the Lakes. Harding Productions. New Waterford, Ohio, 1989.

Runabout Renaissance: The Rebirth of the Wooden Pleasure Boat. Irvine, David (producer). Shelbyville, Michigan: Video-Craft, 1990.

Unpublished Material

Boat Companies of Racine. Manuscript/Scrapbook, In the collections of the Great Lakes Historical Society, Vermilion, Ohio.

Defoe, A. D. *Development of the Defoe Shipbuilding Company.* Bay City, Michigan 1964. In the collections of the Great Lakes Historical Society, Vermilion, Ohio.

Defoe records in the Historical Collections of the Great Lakes, Bowling Green (Ohio) State University.

Hacker Boat Company records, through the courtesy of S. Steven McCready.

151 Pelican class, 33
225 (225-cubic-inch class), 43, 44
Adieu, 20, 26, 27
Adriatic, 24
Aeldcytha, 81
Alagi, 41, 42
American Power Boat Association, 22–25,
   29–31, 35, 41, 43
Anita, 12
Ankle Deep, 20, 21
Ann-A-Bob, 115
Arbib, Richard, 112, 117
Areta II, 65
Arrow, 15
Astor, Vincent, 59
Athena, 69
Au Revoir, 20, 53
Avro, 108
Baby Gar III, 28
Baby Gar IV, 16–18, 28
Baby Gar Jr., 29
Baby Gar Jr., 55
Baby Gars, 27, 28, 54, 55
Baby Reliance, 18, 19
Baby Reliance II, 19, 20
Baby Reliance III, 19, 20, 21
Baby Speed Demon, 19
Baby Speed Demon II, 21
Baby Sure Cure, 20
Baby Zackaroo, 60
Baker, Delphine Dodge, 41
Barat, 95
Barrel-back, 70, 71
Barrett, Lee, 18, 19, 39
Bassett, Glen, 100, 101
Bay City Boats, Inc., 84
Beebe, Jack, 19, 22, 23
Beebe, Martin, 23
Bel Geddes, Norman, 101
Belle Isle Bear Cats, 52, 53, 55, 56
Belle Isle Boat & Engine Company, 53, 54
Betty, 76
Big Chief, 83
Black, Montague, 76
Blackton, J. Stuart, 19–21
Bragg, Caleb, 29
Bruin, 31
Buchanan, Fred, 64
Buddy, 71
Buffalo Launch Club, 32
Burger Boat Company, 82, 83, 94, 114, 115
Burger, Henry E., 114
Burgess, Rosamund, 10
Burgess, Starling, 10
Burwell, 77, 79
Cadet, 58
Capone, Al, 82, 92
Carstairs, Marion Barbara "Betty", 31, 33,
   34, 36
Century Boat Company, 61, 69–72, 100, 106,
   111–113, 115–119
Chapman, Charles F., 23
Chapman, Jean, 49
Chris-Craft, 11, 27, 31, 32, 34, 42, 43,
   52–61, 67–73, 83, 91, 94, 96, 101–109,
   111, 115, 117
Cigarette, 85, 86
Classic runabout, 55, 56
Cleary, Henry J., 13
Cobras, 102, 107
Coll, Harry H., 103
Colonial Boat Works, 107
Comet, 89
Coronado, 98–100
Covana, 67

Criqui, Charles, A., 50
Crouch, George F., 55, 59
Curlew, 67
Day, Thomas Fleming, 81
Dazzle, 57
De Roy, Aaron, 29
Dee Wite, 60, 63
Deed, William, 90
Defoe Boat and Motor Works, 83, 84, 89
Defoe, Fredrick, 83
Defoe, Harry J., 83
Dehaviland, 108
Delphine IV, 40
Delphine IV, 41
Delphine IX, 41
Delphine V, 40
Delphine VII, 41
Detroit Exchange Club, 18
Detroit Launch & Power Company, 53
Detroit Marine-Aero Engine Company, 27, 29
Detroit Yacht Club, 31, 40, 41, 80
Detroit, 80, 81
Di Montelera, Count Theo Rossi, 41
Dilman, Anna, 55, 59, 106
Dispro (Disappearing Propeller Boat Company),
   49, 51, 66
Ditchburn, 24, 25, 29, 30, 35, 59, 64, 65, 67, 68
Ditchburn, Alf, 64
Ditchburn, Herb, 64
Dodge Jr., Horace, 33, 40, 41, 44, 55, 59,
   60, 106
Dolly Durkin, 64
Dolphins, 54, 55
Don, Kaye, 38, 39, 40, 41, 44
Dwight Lumber Company, 63
Eddy Boat Company, 105
Edgar, Sir Mackay, 20, 24
Edison, Thomas, 58
Edward II, 46–48
El Legarto, 41
Eldredge-McInnes, 90
Empress, 71
Esdres, Herni, 33
Estelle II, 34
Estelle IV, 31, 36
Estelle V, 36
Excelsior-France II, 33
Excelsior-France, 33
Fairbanks-Morse, 14
Farr, John B., 53
Fermann, William, 88
Field, Marshall, 85
Firestone, Harvey, 58
Fisher, Carl G., 24, 29, 33, 89
Flying Cloud, 88, 89
Ford, Edsel, 23
Ford, Edward, 80
Ford, Henry, 23, 54
Ford Motor Company, 50, 51, 81
Frances, 86, 88
Gage Marine Corporation, 106
Gar Jr. Flyers, 85, 86
Gar Jr. II, 84, 85
Gar Sr., 86
Gar Wood Industries, see Wood, Garfield A.
Geisha, 14
Gidley, Henry, 49, 50
Gidleyford, 49–51
Globe, 13
Godfather, 52, 53
Gray Marine Motor Company, 51
Gray, William M., 63
Great Lakes Boat Building Corporation, 86,
   87, 94, 95
Greavette Boats Ltd., 64, 67, 68

Greavette, Tom, 43–45, 67
Grebe, Henry C., 94, 95
Grebe, M. L., 95
Greening, Harry, 24, 26, 27, 29, 30, 35, 64, 67
Grew, 50
Gribbens, Joseph, 23
H. C. Minett Boat Works, 64
Hacker Boat Company, 25, 26, 28, 52–55,
   59, 61–63, 69, 70, 89, 95, 105, 106, 110
Hacker, John A., 61, 62
Hacker, John L., 20, 29, 33, 41, 43, 44, 50,
   53–57, 61–69, 76, 84, 88, 89, 91, 92,
   95, 105, 106, 110–113
Hackercraft, 48, 54, 56, 61, 69, 91, 111
Hamersley, L. Gordon, 85, 86
Hand, William H., 89
Harmsworth, Alfred, 23
Harris, 34
Hathor, 10
Havana Special, 84
Hawker, Bert, 36
Hayward, Colonial William, 29, 32
Heather, 114
Hegg, Allan, 112, 113
Henry C. Grebe & Co., 95
Herreshoff Manufacturing Company, 10
Hickory, 9, 10
Higgens, Jay, 23
Hopkins, Mark, 10
Horace E. Dodge Boat Works, 55, 68
Horn, William, 40, 41
Horton, Edward Everett, 48
Hotsy Totsy III, 41, 42
Huber, Bob, 70
Hunt, Fitz, 20, 48
Huskins Boatbuilding Company, 95
Hutchinson, 49, 50, 106, 109, 111
Hutchinson, Charles, 109
Hydroplane, 19–24, 29, 33, 34, 41, 42, 59,
   65, 106, 112
Ida, 11
Impshi, 41, 44
Irwin, 81
Jay, Webb, 26
Jay-Dee II, 42
Jay-Dee III, 43
John I. Thornycroft Ltd., 39
John L. Hacker Co., 106
Johnson, Orlin, 28, 31, 33, 34, 37
Johnston Jr., W. J., 49
Judson, A. L., 22, 23, 24
Junior Gold Cup, 28, 29
Kahlenberg, Otto, 13, 50
Kahlenberg, William, 13, 50
Kehrig Manufacturing Company, 105
Kermath Manufacturing Company, 52, 54
King of Siam, 89, 91
King, E. L., 86
Kingfisher, 86
Kitty Hawk, 20, 53
Kitty Hawk II, 20
Kittyhawk, 50, 51
Knockdown boats, 83, 84
Kosh Machine, 117
Lacy, Volney E., 90, 97
Lady Helen, 28, 33
Lady Helen II, 29, 33
Lafond, John, 13
Lake Georgia Racing Association, 20
Lake Shore Engine Works, 13
Lapstrake boats, 63, 110, 111, 116
Launches, 10–14, 64, 68, 84, 93
Leo III, 61
Leveau, Walter, 92
Lewis, Jim, 106

Lisee, Napoleon, 26, 27, 34, 56–58, 101
Little Miss Canada IV, 44
Little Spitfire, 33
Locke, Dick, 29
Lockpat II, 62
Lozier Motor Company, 78–80
Lozier, H. A., 77, 78, 80
Lutz, Bob, 112
Lyman Boatworks, 63, 69, 70, 95, 100, 102, 106, 110, 111, 114–116
Lyman, Bill, 63, 70, 95, 110, 111
Lyon, Charles P., 106
MacKerer, Bill, 56–59, 91, 96
Mahogany Rose, 116
Mankowski, Count, 20, 21
Maple Leaf IV, 25
Maple Leaf V, 24
Maple Leaf VI, 24, 25
Marold, 81, 86
Mary Jeanne II, 95
Mary K., 88
Matthews Company, 77, 80–82, 86, 93, 107–109, 114
Matthews, Carl, 109
Matthews, Scott J., 77–80, 109
McCready, C. P., 54, 62, 66
McCready, S. Dudley, 54, 62, 66
McLellan, Lieutenant C. H., 13
McMillian, John G., 114, 115
Meiers, Bernard, C., 90, 97
Miller, Fredrick Milo, 80
Milot, John, 21, 22
Minett, H. C., 64, 67
Minett-Shields, 64, 65, 67
Miss America, 21, 24, 25
Miss America II, 24–26
Miss America III, 33
Miss America IV, 33
Miss America V, 33, 35–37
Miss America VI, 33, 34
Miss America VII, 30, 34–37
Miss America VIII, 36, 38, 39
Miss America IX, 34, 36, 38, 39
Miss America X, 37–43
Miss Britain III, 42, 43
Miss Canada II, 43
Miss Canada III, 44, 45
Miss Detroit, 18, 21, 22
Miss Detroit II, 18
Miss Detroit III, 23
Miss Detroit V, 24
Miss Detroit VII, 33
Miss Detroit Power Boat Association, 21, 42
Miss England, 35, 37
Miss England II, 36, 38, 39
Miss England III, 39, 40
Miss Liberty II, 86
Miss Los Angeles, 20
Miss Mary, 41
Miss Miami, 24
Miss Minneapolis, 22
Miss Packard, 31
Miss Pepsi, 106, 112
Miss Syndicate, 33
Misty Chris, 103
MIT II, 20
Mollica, Anthony, 100
Moodie, R. R., 80
Moore, Philip, 92
Morehead, W. C., 94
Mulford, O. J., 50, 51
My Sin, 42
My Sweetie, 106, 111
Naiad, 11
Nepenthe, 76
Never Again, 116
Newman, Frank, 70
Nordlinger Trophy, 20
North Star II, 93
Notre Dame, 41, 42
Olds, Ransom E., 88

Onward, 80
Oregon Kid, 20
Orlo, 27
Orlo II, 27
Overlakes Freight Corporation, 111
Ox, 10
Packard Baby Gar, 28
Packard Chriscraft, 21, 29
Packard Chriscraft II, 31, 33
Packard Chriscraft III, 31
Packard Motor Car Company, 24, 28, 39
Packards at Speed, 39
Page, Charles E., 51, 52
Pam, 88
Pardon Me, 106, 111
Peabody, C. H., 13
Pilgrim, 94
Port Carling Boat Works, 64, 66–68
Power Boating, 96
Powered skiff, 49, 51, 66, 67
Pugh, Wallace, 20
Purcell, Irene, 50
Purdy Boat Company, 33, 89
Racine Boat Manufacturing Company, 10, 13, 14
Rainbow, 24, 26, 27, 29, 64, 67
Rainbow III, 25, 26, 27, 29, 30, 31
Rainbow IV, 30, 31, 35
Rainbow VII, 35
Rand Jr., James H., 33
Ranger, 82
Raven, 116
Rebel, 54
Reconstruction Finance Corporation, 69, 70
Reid, Lorna, 43–45
Reis, George, 41
Restless, 32
Reynolds Aluminum, 114
Richardson Boat Company, 89, 90, 92–94, 96, 97, 106–108
Richardson, G. Reid, 94, 106
Ringling, John, 30, 86
Roamer Corporation, 102
Robinson Marine Construction Company, 88, 90–92, 95, 96, 97
Robinson, Glen, 91
Rochester Boat Company, 55, 58, 90, 91, 97
Rodengen, Jeffrey, 73
Roosevelt, President Franklin Delano, 45
Rosewill, 89
Ross, David, 115
Rowdy, 33
Royce, James, 65
Rudder, The, 14, 15, 79, 81
Ruffolo, Jim, 115
Rumrunners, 82, 84
Ruspoli, Prince Carlo, 37
Ryan, Baldy, 19–21
Ryerson Steel, 10
S2 Yachts, Inc., 118
Sail and Sweep, 80
Sailaway, 93
Samovars, 11
Sanford, W. E., 11
Scott-Paine, Hubert, 42, 43
Scout, 90
Scripps Motor Company, 51, 80
Scripps, William E., 51, 80
Sea Maid, 70, 72, 111, 115, 116
SeaBirds, 66, 67
Seagull, 88, 90, 91
Seagull, 95
Seeber, Vernon, 83
Segrave, Henry, 36, 37, 38
Semi-displacement boats, 49, 50, 63, 65, 81
Sentimental Lady, 102
Shadow F, 89
Shields, Bryson, 64
Show Girl, 50
Silver Arrows, 103, 109
Sirocco, 113

Skit, 20
Slickcraft, 115, 118
Slikkers, Leon, 115, 118
Smith, Bernard, 20, 57, 73, 103
Smith, Catherine, 57
Smith, Chris, 107
Smith, Christopher Columbus, 11, 18–22, 24, 25, 27, 28, 31, 37, 42, 54–59, 71, 73, 106, 107
Smith, Hamilton, 103
Smith, Harvey, 107
Smith, Jay, 19, 34, 57, 73, 103
Smith, Owen, 57, 103
Smith-Ryan Boat Company, 19, 20
Special Yacht Tender, 59
Spectre, Peter, 63
Spide, 115
Spitfire, 33
Spitfire IV, 33
Spitfire V, 33
Splish Splash, 109
Stephensen, Luke, 71, 73
Sterling Engine Company, 50
Strawbridge, James, 76
Sunbeam-Despujols, 24
Sweet Louise, 72
Sylvan Jr., 49
Tacoma Boatbuilding, 115
Tahoe Tessie, 72
Tait, Colonial A. W., 25
Tamarask, 94
Teddy, 31
Terrible, 48
Thompson Boat Company, 105
Thunderbird, 74–76, 95
Thunderbolt, 70
Tiara, 115, 117–119
Top Hat, 66
Toronto, 48
Torrey, H. N., 85
Union Gas Engineering Company, 13,
United Marine, 108
V, 37
Vamaheka, 79
Van Blerck, Joseph, 15, 51, 52
Van Blerck Motor Company, 15, 53
Van Patten, Doug, 44
Venice Regatta, 36
Vernon Jr., 833
Via Water, 89
Viking, 30
Vincent, Col. J. G., 26, 28, 29, 31–33, 41
Virginia, 114
Wakefield, Lord, 38, 39, 41
Walker, Harrington F., 88
Wampum, 60
Warner, H. H., 10
Wasp II, 86
Watercars, 55, 57
Waterman, 15
Whip-O-Will, Jr., 23, 24
White Cap, 14
Whitehouse, G. H., 83
Whittell, George, 95
Wiehn, Fred E., 111
Wild Horses, 22
Wiley, Fred, 112
Wills, C. H., 81
Wilmur II, 65
Wilson, Harold, 43, 44, 45
Wood, Garfield A., 18, 20–29, 31–43, 54–58, 60, 69–71, 84–86, 94, 100, 101, 106, 111
Wood, Logan, 100
Wood, Phil, 31, 37
Wright, Orville, 50, 51
Wrigley, Philip K., 86, 94
Yacht & Power Company, 50
Yachtsmen's Association of America, 23
Yamaha, 113